March of America Facsimile Series

Number 70

A Visit to Texas

A Visit to Texas

ANN ARBOR

UNIVERSITY MICROFILMS, INC.

A Subsidiary of Xerox Corporation

Foreword

Before Texas won its independence from Mexico in 1836, some 25,000 to 30,000 persons from the United States had already poured into the region. Land companies operating from the United States were at least partly responsible for the influx. Claiming to hold large tracts of land in Texas, the companies induced many Americans and Europeans to purchase lands from them. The anonymous author of *A Visit To Texas: Being The Journal Of A Traveller* had purchased 20,000 acres from one such company and went to Texas in 1831 to take possession of his estate. Soon after arriving he made the unhappy discovery that he had been swindled—the Mexican Republic refused to recognize his purchase. Upon his return to the United States and after a visit to the office of the land company in New York where he received "neither remuneration nor sympathy for my fruitless expense and disappointments," he published in 1834 an account of his experiences. He intended his book to serve as a warning to others who might similarly be misled by the false claims of the land companies. His book helped acquaint Americans with the then unfamiliar land and people of Texas.

The author, who came from the northern section of the United States, reached New Orleans in March, 1831. There he boarded a ship bound for the Brazos River, the same river on which Stephen Austin had established the first permanent Anglo-American settlement in Texas ten years before. The author's first impressions of the country were generally favorable. It seemed ideal for settlement. There were no obstacles to travel, no forests to clear, and the soil was rich, "often of almost incalculable fertility." Bounteous harvests were virtually assured with minimum effort.

However after several days in Texas the author began to hear disquieting reports: the Mexican government was refusing to honor the grants of the American land companies. Not long after, he learned that the reports were all too true. The money he had paid in New York meant nothing in Texas. He could still acquire Texas land, to be sure—in fact he could acquire a quarter league of unappropriated land from the Mexican authorities. But only "on condition of professing the Roman Catholic religion, becoming a citizen of the Republic of Mexico, and residing on the soil for six years." It was the religious requirement which troubled him most, for he was convinced that Roman Catholicism was by nature inimical to republicanism and "that both cannot have at once the ascendency."

He wished to return to the United States immediately but found that there would be a wait of some duration until a ship sailed. Consequently he decided to see more of the country while waiting. In his travels he came across many others who had been deceived by the land companies. Often whole families of emigrants from the United States and Europe were stranded, without funds to go back home. He observed too that many of the Americans coming into Texas were fugitives from justice. It was somewhat disconcerting, he said, to sit down to breakfast and find that four of those at the table were murderers, as he did on one occasion. His impressions of the Mexicans were for the most part uncomplimentary. They appeared to be a "timid and inefficient race" he thought.

A map and a meteorological journal for the summer of 1831 accompany the text. Useful for an understanding of Texas in this period are: David B. Edward, *The History of Texas; or The Emigrant's, Farmer's and Politician's Guide* (Cincinnati, 1836) and Mattie A. Hatcher, *Letters of an Early American Traveller: Mary Austin Holley; Her Life and Her Works* (Dallas, 1933). Some background for conditions in Texas before the republic is contained in William R. Hogan, *The Texas Republic* (Norman, 1946).

VISIT TO TEXAS:

BEING

THE JOURNAL OF A TRAVELLER

THROUGH THOSE PARTS MOST

INTERESTING TO AMERICAN SETTLERS.

WITH DESCRIPTIONS OF SCENERY, HABITS, &C. &C.

NEW YORK:

GOODRICH & WILEY, 124 BROADWAY

1834.

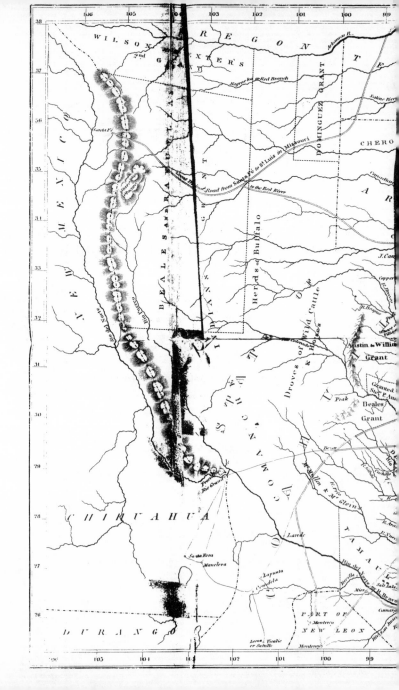

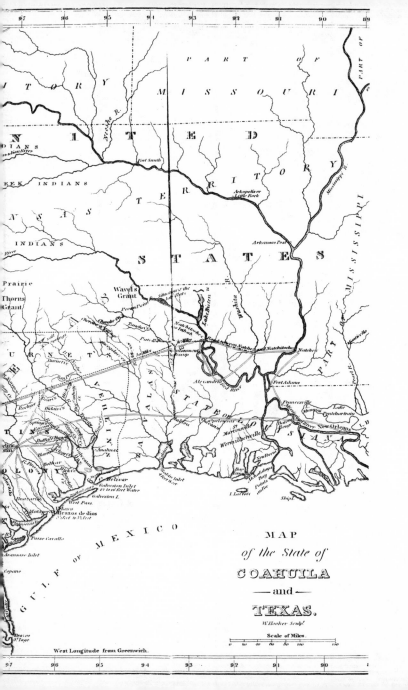

MAP

of the State of

COAHUILA

— and —

TEXAS.

W. Hooker Sculp.

Scale of Miles.

West Longitude from Greenwich.

MAHLON DAY, PRINTER, 374 PEARL-STREET.

CONTENTS.

CONTENTS.

Page.

VISIT TO TEXAS.

CHAPTER I.

Departure from New Orleans.—Passengers.—Galveston Island.—
The bays and Coast of Texas.—Wild Fowl.—Landing at the
Brazos.

EARLY in the month of March, 1831, I reached
New Orleans from the Northern States, on my way
to Texas. My principal object was to examine the
condition of a large tract of land I had purchased of
the Galveston Bay and Texas Land Company, and
to ascertain its value to settlers from the United
States, by personal observation, as well as to satisfy
myself concerning the soundness of the title which
I had obtained.

There was a vessel at that time preparing to sail
for Brazoria, a place on the river Brazos; and I took
passage on board. After stipulating for the price of
twenty dollars, and providing myself with a few
conveniences for the voyage, I embarked with fifty-
three other passengers, of different descriptions and
colors. The sloop Majesty, in which we sailed,

1

commanded by Captain Spear, was taken in tow by the steamboat Livingston, and went through the North West Pass about 7 o'clock in the morning. Our cargo had been selected for Brazoria by a young merchant of that place, who was on board, and consisted of flour, provisions, clothes, &c.

I had sought in vain for any satisfactory information concerning the country to which I was bound, before leaving New Orleans; and was but little more fortunate in my enquiries among the passengers, most of whom were going to live in Texas. Among these were an old Tennessean and his wife with their sons, two young men, who were going "to hunt land," as the familiar term is for exploring new regions, for a place to form a settlement. There was also a very intelligent man from Alabama, who had several negroes with him, going to take up his abode in Texas: but he had nothing to communicate concerning the country, except some very favorable general accounts he had received from friends. On reaching New Orleans he had learnt for the first time, that slaves cannot be held in the Mexican territory, and had taken measures which had been recommended to him, to evade the general law of abolition, which does so much honor to the patriots of that republic. He had obtained their attested signatures to articles of indenture, by which they bound themselves to serve him for ninety-nine years. He counselled another man, who was on board with his wife and several slaves, to do the same, and gave them such instructions as were necessary to be regarded to render the pretended agreement binding on the negroes.

I learned from conversation with the captain of the vessel, that he once sailed with Gibbs, the notorious pirate, who had been brought into New-York a short time before our sailing, but whose confessions had not at that time been made. He assured me that he was a man of a most profligate and desperate character ; and that he entertained no doubt at all of his being guilty of such acts of piracy and murder as were charged against him, and many more than were yet known.

On the 12th of March we discovered land, which presented only a low, uniform appearance, on which it would be impossible to distinguish one spot from another. The most experienced navigators of the coast are often at a loss hereabouts. On the following day we passed Galveston Island, which extends sixty miles, and differs in nothing from the land just mentioned, except that in one spot, viz. near the western extremity, are three low trees growing near the water, which, although of very diminutive size, are visible from a great distance on account of their loneliness, and serve as a convenient landmark in clear weather.

We kept down the coast until we arrived off the mouth of the Brazos, near which we began to dis-

cover something of the country in the interior.
This was an extensive plain, scarcely elevated above
the level of the Ocean, varied in some parts with
wood, but without a single elevation of the surface·
A pilot came down to the shore, and we stood near
the land to receive him.   The sloop was got in over
the bar without much difficulty, though she struck
two or three times, as she drew five feet of water.
The water on the bar varies from four to six feet.

The bays, harbors, and rivers of Texas, are generally obstructed at their mouths by the meeting of
their currents with the waves in the gulf.   According to Mrs. Holley's "Texas," Sabine Lake, on the
eastern frontier, has but six feet of water at its mouth,
and shoals within.   Galveston Bay has obstructions
not only at its mouth, but at Redfish bar, and above,
which preclude the navigation of Trinity and San
Jacinto rivers, in vessels of any considerable size,
and sometimes forbid it entirely in the former.   The
bar of the Brazos is said to be only about four rods
wide, and easily removeable.   Matagorda Bay is
shoal, though it has twelve feet of water at its entrance ; with only three or three and a half feet at
the mouths of its two rivers, Colorado and La Baca.
The Colorado is also impassable ten miles above
Matagorda, there being a raft, or fixed mass of timber lying in the channel.   The San Bernard and
Caney's creeks are very shoal at their mouths.   The
bay of Aransaso has seven feet at the entrance, and

a pretty good depth within, as has also Neuces bay. Here are the Irish grants, where Irish Colonies are to be formed.

Before our vessel reached the point, four of the passengers including myself, took the boat intending to land. After rowing a short time, we perceived that the surf ran high upon the beach, and that a landing would be difficult. We had also by this time discovered that we were all but poor oarsmen; but nothing remained for us but to keep the boat's head as well as possible towards the shore. We had however, no sooner reached the breakers, than she swung round in spite of us, and instantly overset, throwing us all into the water. We scrambled among the waves and the undertow, and with difficulty gained the land, after spending some time in hauling the boat upon the beach. Crossing the narrow point not far from its extremity, we soon reached the house of Captain Cotton, where a flag was flying. It stands on the bank of the Brazos river, and is an inn, for the accommodation of passengers landing here, though a mere log house. The owner was formerly editor of a Mexican Gazette.

From this place we had an extensive prospect. Although the spot is but little higher than the surface of the water, the country around is so low, and so perfectly flat, that the eye embraced an extent of many miles towards the interior, as well as up and

1*

down the sea-coast. The surface was green, as the
season was already advanced so far that the grass
had grown about six inches; and the trees were
well covered with leaves, forming groves and in some
places woods of considerable extent, especially along
the banks of the river, which was seen to take two
or three great bends within a few miles of us.
Nearer at hand, and on both sides, were several
sheets of water, spreading over considerable tracts of
the level ground, and communicating with the sea.
These offered us at first sight a promise of abundant
sport, for we saw multitudes of fowl in different
places, both near and distant, and the country is
abundant in game. Although the soil was sandy,
the general aspect of the country was verdant and
agreeable, bearing a general resemblance to that
around New Orleans, except in its total want of
inhabitants; for although the cultivation was entirely neglected, it looked as if cultivated. Not a dwelling, except the inn, was any where in sight, nor a
single vessel, except our sloop. This was soon
taken up the river about a mile, and there brought
to anchor.

This, I was informed, is a fair specimen of the
entire coast of Texas. From one extremity to the
other there is not an elevation, nor any variety of
aspect. The surface is low and flat, but destitute of
marshes, so that a cart might almost any where come
down to the edge of the water.

The eastern part of Texas, which we were entering—that is, from the Sabine river, the boundary of the United States, to the San Jacinto, a little westward from us, is regarded as the best part of the territory. It is well watered by navigable rivers and mill streams, and supplied with valuable timber, which will furnish much lumber.

There are as yet however but few inhabitants. Nacogdoches, 60 miles from the frontier, the principal town in that direction, was yet insignificant in the amount of its population. It was at first a Spanish military post, and afterwards inhabited by a small population. The inhabitants were driven into Louisiana about the year 1820, by Spanish troops, but three years after the resettlement began. It was now protected by a small number of Mexican soldiers, which was soon afterwards increased, as the government were then jealous of the United States, or affected to be so. A few scattering settlers are found in that tract of country : but the colonization laws forbid any settlement to be made within twenty leagues of the frontier of the United States, unless two thirds of the inhabitants be Mexicans.

There were ten or twelve puny, dark complexioned men, at Captain Cotton's in an uniform, who I learnt were Mexican soldiers, stationed there to enforce the revenue laws. The state of the Mexican Republic being at that time very unhappy, through the military despotism under the Vice President Bustamente, and the prospect of internal disturbance, it was not so surprising that an advanced post on this distant frontier, should be left with a very slender guard. The approach of no open enemy was to be apprehended from this quarter, although it was very evident that the party in power were hostile to the principles of the United States, opposed to its influence, and extremely jealous of the moral ascendency which our countrymen were rapidly gaining in this province by emigration.

CHAPTER II.

ON the following morning, I was roused by the
cry of "Deer in sight;" and from the deck we saw
distinctly several deer feeding in the Prairie on the
western side of the river, about half a mile from the
bank. They appeared so confident in the security,
and fed so carelessly, that I set off immediately with
my gun, indulging no small hopes of procuring a
supply of fresh meat for at least a part of the ship's
company. My plan was, to proceed quietly along
until I should get rather to the South West of them,
and then approach ; for the river took an abrupt turn
to the westward about a mile north of me, and there
I thought I should be able to pen up my game, if
they should take alarm before my near approach. I
confess my ignorance of deer hunting, which indeed
will be evident enough to an experienced sportsman
from my manner of proceeding. After walking a
short time, and long before I had thought any particular precaution was necessary to prevent them from

observing me, they suddenly started, and after running a few minutes disappeared. I then hurried on, expecting to find them concealed under the bank of the river; and ran over the smooth and grassy level, till I was out of breath; but, much to my disappointment, I could find nothing of them on the shore. After looking about a little time, I perceived several dark spots in the water, nearly a mile off, which proved to be my deer, swimming for a distant point of land, and leaving me in a mortifying predicament under the observation of all the sloops' company.

I was very much struck with the uniformity of the surface in the Prairie; which I had often heard of so particularly, but never observed before. I had now run a mile or more over it, without meeting a single irregularity or obstacle, a stone, a pebble, a bush, or even a shrub. Scarcely a blade of grass seemed to rise above the ordinary height, which, as I have before remarked, was about six inches. And thus this extensive plain, neglected by man, and tended only by the hand of nature, presented a surface as level as the most carefully rolled garden-walk, and was covered with a coat of green as uniform as a smooth shaven lawn, or a vast sheet of velvet. And this scene was not confined to a small vale or meadow, or bounded by a range of neighboring hills: but stretched off to a vast distance on almost every side, on the one hand seeming to melt into the Gulf of Mexico, and on the other to meet the horizon. There was nothing elevated, or rough, or wild, to contrast with the flat surface of green; and after a few moments spent in contemplating the plain, finding it varied only by the distant groves which were seen towards the north, the mind feels a kind of surprise at finding, that the senses are almost useless where there is so little to give them exercise. Such were some of my feelings at the first sight of a Prairie.

There were some objects however which attracted my attention, particularly towards the South: for multitudes of water fowl were clustered together near the shore, as vast flocks of them were continually in the air. Having lost all hope of larger game, and having no particular disposition to return to the vessel, while the recollection of my defeat in the deer expedition was so fresh, I shouldered my gun, and bent my course towards the shore of the Gulf, and towards a spot where the fowl seemed to be most numerous.

After a walk, that proved somewhat oppressive on account of the heat, (the thermometer was at 75° at Anahuac at noon that day,) I reached the shore of a pond, or lagoon, which, communicating with the Gulf by a narrow opening, overflowed a considerable extent of land, and offered a convenient retreat to thousands of wild ducks, geese, brandt and other fowl. These were far less shy than the game I had before pursued, and soon offered me opportunities to try my powder and shot. There were different kinds of fowl which I had never met with before, and one of great size particularly attracted my attention. It was standing in the shallow water, near the land, and must have weighed forty or fifty pounds. By proper caution I got within a moderate distance of this overgrown mark, which I viewed at my leisure from the spot where I was concealed by the bank; and then, taking good aim, drew the trigger. My gun however missed fire; and the bird, spreading its wings at the click of the lock, was soon beyond my reach. Turning round, I now, to my dismay, discovered that the sloop had hoisted sail, and was already moving up the Brazos, with a favoring breeze which had unexpectedly sprung up; so, taking several ducks which I had shot, I set off in great haste to overtake it. There was no probability that the Captain would heave to for me, unless he could do it with a prospect of little loss of time; and instead of directing my course towards the place where the vessel then was, I inclined much further towards the left, to reach the river at a distant bend, where I hoped to arrive as soon as the sloop. To do this however required great exertion; for the breeze was strong enough to carry her along pretty rapidly, and the prospect of a long walk over the Prairie was of a most discouraging nature. I pushed on however, as fast as I could, worried with vexation at perceiving that my companions displayed no disposition to wait for me; and at length effected my object, after a walk, or rather almost a run, of five miles. I was very happy to find myself once more on board, after the prospect I had had of more solitude than I desired.

The Brazos river is generally about 150 feet wide, and 20 or 30 feet deep. It is remarkably crooked: so much so that no one wind will take a vessel up to Brazoria, the place to which we were bound. Fortunately for us, we had men enough on board to obviate this difficulty; and by sending a number of them on shore with a rope at every bad turn, we were able to pursue our course without delay. Not long after I had got on board, which was at noon, we began to approach the timber land; and we found the banks in some places more elevated and irregular, but without any signs of cultivation or inhabitants. I learnt that the open Prairies extended to within a short distance of the stream. The soil was light and poor until we reached a place called McNeil's Landing, or Marion, about fifteen miles, or half the distance to Brazoria, where, however, was no dwelling of any kind. One of the oldest estates in this part of the country, (that of Mr. McNeil,) is situated a few miles westward, in the interior, near the river St. Bernard, whose general course is nearly parallel with that of the Brazos. At this landing the cotton raised by Mr. McNeil is shipped for New Orleans; and in the year 1830 the amount

2

of this article yielded to that estate alone was worth no less than five thousand dollars. The estate of Mr. Westall is also a few miles from the Brazos on that side: but with these exceptions there were no habitations in the country within some miles of us.

After observing something new, in a strange country, one is apt to inquire whether it is likely to be often met with in future. I had now been upon a Prairie for the first time: but I had to anticipate a more familiar acquaintance with them. Indeed it was most probable I should often travel, and possibly I might sometimes be obliged to sleep upon them. The beautiful and unvarying level on which I now found myself, had no near limits. The truth is, the entire southern part of Texas is one vast Prairie; and in the northern regions of this extensive province is another, which, stretching to the boundary of the United States, is lost in the Valley of the Mississippi and its western tributaries. That which lay before me extended north about seventy miles without interruption, except near some of the streams.

These regions, which present no obstacle to the traveller in any direction, except where they are crossed by streams, and whose soil is generally rich, and often of almost incalculable fertility, present superior attractions to colonists. No forests are to be cleared away; and yet, in many places, there is sufficient wood for the limited necessities created by the climate. How many attractions does this splendid country appear at first sight to offer to a settler from our cold and Northern States! No rocky and barren ledges to lie waste forever, no steep acclivities to be tilled or to be climbed over; no provision to be made for the housing of cattle; no raising, cutting, curing, removing, stowing or feeding out of winter fodder; not even the construction of hay stacks; much less the erection of barns or stables for crops and stock. How difficult it is to a northerner to bear in mind the reality, that all these great features of soil, climate and rural life in his own country are here to be dispensed with! He naturally inquires, "What then can remain for the industrious man to do?" The whole business of raising cattle is of course reduced, as it was in the land of Canaan, to the simple operation of letting them take care of themselves, eat, drink and fatten on the rich pastures and under the genial climate, until the owner chooses to claim tribute of their flesh, hide and horns. Tillage is also reduced almost to its simplest form : for cotton is packed as soon as picked, and immediately transported to market; and as to the grain necessary for the colonist's use, although the scarcity of mills is at present a great inconvenience, the planting is often effected without preparing the ground, and the rearing always without hoeing. Vegetables are generally still more easily procured, and that in superabundance : for after having been once sowed, many kinds of useful kitchen plants and roots propagate

themselves. This is the case with pumpkins, sweet
potatoes, and several other vegetables; and some of
them have been found greatly to improve in quality
from year to year, even when thus entirely left to
the care of nature. It is remarkable of the common
North American or Irish potatoe, that when cultivated here it becomes sweet, like the Southern or
Carolina potatoe.

The Prairies or levels of Texas may be generally
described under two heads: 1st. The Southern or
those on the coast, and 2d. The Northern, or interior.
I am now nearly in the middle of the former, which
extends from the river San Jacinto to that of Guadaloupe, and about eighty miles inland, and beyond
the latter river to the Nuces, thirty or forty miles
back. The Eastern coast division, is generally well
watered, being crossed by the rivers La Baca, Colorado and San Bernard, as well as the Brazos, with
many smaller streams, and containing abundance of
springs. Though apparently a dead flat, the country
descends so much towards the Gulf of Mexico, that
it is well drained, the streams being rapid, and the
land neither overspread by ponds nor morasses, nor
liable to inundations. The want of stones, for
building and other purposes, and the abundance of
musquetoes and other insects are seriously felt. The
moderate prevalence of bilious fevers throughout
this region is an objection, though not a very important one, against settlements here, as they are far

less fatal than in some parts of the United States.
The proximity to the coast and streams to some
extent navigable, and of course the facilities of com-
munication with distant regions, as well as the
greater progress of settlements, are among the advantages of the southern over the northern Prairies.
All this extensive tract, except a narrow strip west
of La Baça river, is comprehended in Austin's
Colony.

The western and smaller division of the coast
level or Prairie land, extends, as before remarked,
only about half as far inland as that first described :
but it is more elevated, has even richer herbage, and
is preferred on the score of salubrity. The musquito
grass which overspreads the ground is green all the
year. Among the timber is also found the musquito
tree, which is very useful for fences and fuel. The
greater part of this valuable region is covered by the
grants made to De Leon and Power, and is destined
for Irish settlements. It extends to the limits of
Texas on the coast, and embraces several large bays,
peninsulas and islands.

The northern levels or Prairies are of considerable
extent in the boundaries of Texas : lying along the
head streams of Brazos river, and extending northward become identified with those vast plains between
the Rocky Mountains and the Mississippi. But they
are little known, and as yet scarcely within the view
of colonists, though doubtless destined at some future

time, to support a numerous population. That region, as when crossed by Captain Zebulon Pike in 1807, is still traversed by herds of buffalo, deer, and horses and Indians; particularly the Comanches, who are wild and savage.

The country intermediate between these great levels, is swelling, (or "rolling," as it is here called,) adjacent to the Prairies, and mountainous in the middle. The rolling country extends northward, in some parts one, in others two hundred miles, where it reaches the mountains. It is remarkably salubrious, well supplied with stone, abounds in streams and springs, with timber of various kinds, as well as fine pasturage, beautiful and varied scenery, and is nearly free from troublesome insects. The soil, like that of the Prairies, is generally a deep, dark mould, but the streams are usually bordered by tracts of alluvial land, which yield a variety of timber. The climate and soil are the most favorable to vines, as well as sheep and horses, and as much so as any part of the country to fruits and grain, pigs and oxen. Sugar and long staple cotton, however, will not grow there.

When one listens to the accounts he hears of the fertile regions around him, and sees with his own eyes evidence of the truth of much that he is told, he still finds it difficult to carry with him full credit in the facts, and is often inclined to question over and over again the reality of the tales he has been told. Especially does it seem hard to imagine that such boundless regions of almost unexampled fertility, stretch off to so great a distance beyond us, where the foot of a civilized man has hardly ever been placed. On the contrary, the inconveniences, privations and disappointments which in such a land of beauty and fertility necessarily await the stranger, are apt to force themselves frequently and intelligibly upon his notice. Although the trials to which a new settler must be exposed are fewer and less dangerous than those encountered in our northerly regions, they are still considerable; and every colonist should prepare to meet them. Some of the greatest inconveniences, it is evident, must arise from the scarcity of inhabitants. A mere glance at a vast Prairie, with the idea of living upon it alone, is enough to impress a man with the importance of society to a social being, and the value of that mutual assistance which men give and receive in communities. But yet there are many persons who are habituated to solitude, and while with their families, never feel lonely; and of such must in a great measure consist the colonists of Texas.

The scenes around me afforded certainly a noble view, even for a spectator personally uninterested in the soil: but to the proprietor of a vast tract, like myself, a finer could hardly be imagined. I had doubtless made a judicious purchase; and in what a country! How nobly would twenty thousand acres look, wherever I might determine to locate my estate! I should feel perfectly satisfied with land like this, but, as I had determined to see something of the land in the length and breadth of it, I concluded to suspend my decision for the present. As however this kind of country, as I was assured, extended sixty or seventy miles in depth back from the whole coast east of this, that is, through the southern part of the Company's lands, I could have no difficulty whatever in selecting a section with which I should be satisfied, even if I should be disappointed with the quality of the land in the interior. Twenty thousand acres! Twenty thousand acres! What an estate! How many cattle and human inhabitants would it be able to support!

No wonder that settlers in such a country should acquire feelings of independence and liberality, thought I. Nature is bountiful to the inhabitant, and he can afford to be liberal without impoverishing himself. How strange would it probably appear, to some of those who hear the propositions of the Galveston Bay and Texas Land Company with coldness, if they could see this scene, that they have given the subject no more attention.

I had these agreeable reflections to make, as I passed up the Brazos, expecting on my arrival at Brazoria, to obtain all information necessary to guide me to some of the best of the Company's land, to apply to the Company's surveyor to locate me twen-

ty thousand acres wherever I should direct him, and
to receive a clear and indisputable title from the
Company's agents. A vessel had already arrived,
near the end of February, in Galveston Bay, with
several agents, and a number of emigrants to begin
a settlement on the extensive and valuable lands,
which, as was understood, the Company had full
authority to colonize, sell, or otherwise to dispose of
as they might judge proper. Another vessel was
expected soon, and their beginnings appeared to
presage and guarantee a rapid settlement of the
country. I had been given to understand, as I
thought on good authority, that surveyors and agents
would be found on the spot, under the direction of
the Company, ready to act, and able to perform all
the stipulations which I had been led to suppose
they had bound themselves to in the disposal of the
scrip which I had purchased, and a certificate of
which I had brought out with me ; a sufficient testimony of my claim to the land I had paid for.

Above this place the soil appeared much better,
being black and very deep ; and the surface was still
covered with forests of a variety of trees, though not
very different in their general appearance from those
in more northern regions. The cotton tree, which
is abundant, was new to me : but it is neither beautiful nor valuable ; in form resembling the Lombardy
poplar, and in respect to texture its timber may be
compared with the same.

CHAPTER III.

WE reached Brazoria at about five o'clock. As the
settlement of the place had been commenced but
about twelve months before, little was to be looked
for more than what we found. The village contained about thirty houses, all of logs except three of
brick and two or three framed, and several more
were building. It is laid out in squares of an eighth
of an acre. The river was now about twenty feet
lower than the street, but is swollen every year so
much during the season of floods, as to rise nearly
to the same level, and indeed sometimes overflows a
part of it. The soil was here, as below, very rich
bottom land, black, and 20 feet deep. It is probable
that Brazoria will be the head of sloop navigation :
for although the river above is for some distance deep
enough for vessels of that class, its crooked course
presents a great objection to proceeding any further
up the channel unless with oars. Lots of one-eighth
of an acre sold at from twenty to one hundred and
forty dollars. Brazoria is thirty miles up the river,
but 45 by its crooked course.

I took lodgings at the house of Mr. William Austin; son of the father of American settlers in Texas, Moses Austin. The house was of a very simple construction and plain materials, and may be given as a pretty fair specimen of most of the best houses in the country. I shall therefore be excused for introducing here a description of such a house, with a brief account of the manner in which we were accommodated. Two square houses, about fifteen feet apart, are constructed of logs, well fitted together by deep mortices cut at their ends, where they meet to form the corners. Each of these buildings has a door in the middle, on the side facing inwards; and the space between them being covered over by a roof, a broad passage is left, sheltered indeed above, but quite open at both ends. Add floors to the two houses, or apartments, a few windows closing with wooden shutters and destitute of glass, with a place for a fire in the northern one, and a hole through the roof for the smoke, and you have a description of the principal hotel in Brazoria. The furniture was of the plainest description, and such as barely to serve the most necessary purposes of thirty boarders: for that was the number with whom I found myself associated on entering the mansion. The regular price was four dollars a week; and for transient travellers a dollar a day.

In so new a settlement, where much has already been accomplished, where much more is in prospect,

and where every thing assumes an encouraging
appearance, and every person is under the excitement
of animating hopes, inconveniencies like these are
easily overlooked. The company were cheerful,
conversation was lively, our arrival brought new
subjects of attraction and enquiry to all, and the
time passed very pleasantly. The wife of our host
I found, was an intelligent lady from New-York;
and her care furnished us with excellent food considering the disadvantages of the place, while her
arrangements afforded us more comfort and convenience than we could have expected, in a habitation
so disproportioned to our numbers. Our table was
set on the ground, in the open passage of the house;
while our mattresses were spread at night on the
floor of the southern apartment. In order to place
thirty men in a horizontal position, on a space about
twenty feet square, and each upon a separate bed,
required no small care and calculation ; yet there
we laid ourselves down, as on the floor of a steamboat, and slept soundly till morning.

Mr. John Austin, the first settler of Brazoria,
went there in 1828. The place for the village had
been since cleared of the forest trees which then
overspread the country, and at the time of my visit,
they had been cut away to about the distance of
half a mile. Beyond that line, every thing was
still wild, and in the state of nature. The surface
is almost entirely level; and such is the want of

every species of land-mark, that I was informed that the inhabitants could not venture any considerable distance into the woods in a cloudy or misty day, for fear lest they should lose their way. The most expert woodsman, it was thought, would find himself at fault, for the want of such means as the forest usually affords for determining the points of the compass. What renders the dangers still greater, is the frequency of cane brakes, or tracts of land overgrown with the long reeds of which we make fishing poles in the Northern States. These canes there grow in some places among the forest trees, so thick as to render a passage through them inconvenient : and are often found occupying alone a considerable tract, almost impenetrable by man, and rising so high as to shut out the view of the sky, as well as of every terrestrial object. It was a novelty to me to examine these singular tracts of ground, so unlike every thing which I had seen elsewhere : tall, slender, and graceful rods, growing up rapidly to the height of twenty or twenty-five feet in a single season, affording food to the roving cattle when green, becoming hard, stiff, and durable when dried and preserved, but falling to the ground and perishing when left to themselves, to be succeeded by another similar crop in a few months.

We had an opportunity to judge of the correctness of the reports we had heard, concerning the risk of straying in the forest, at the expense of one of our fellow passengers, a young man from one of the Southern States. He had incautiously taken a walk into the forest; and, on attempting to return, was lost. He was missed by some of his companions, who made such exertions as they could to find him; and these proving unsuccessful, we fired guns occasionally in the night, to inform him of the direction in which he was from Brazoria, and to prevent him at least from straying any further. He did not return that night, but spent it in the woods, and found his way back in the morning.

I was not able to obtain much information in relation to the country, from most of the persons I met with at Brazoria. This was owing partly to the fact, that not a small portion of the people were new-comers from the United States, and partly to the rapid changes taking place in the province. Beside this, every individual like myself, had his mind chiefly occupied with his own concerns; and where every thing was in a state of activity, there was little time, as there were few opportunities, to collect information on other subjects.

There were several shops in the village, in which I found a great variety of articles exposed for sale, though no very large quantity of merchandise in any of them. They sold at very fair prices.

I had some conversation with Mr. Austin on the purchase of land I had made in New-York, but the result was not such as to afford me much gratification.

On the contrary, he regarded the certificate I held, and the scrip which it represented, as of no value whatever. He was confident that the government would never recognise the right claimed by the company, of giving titles to the land; for, as he said, it had not even been conferred upon the empresarios, from whom they pretended to have received it. He had already seen several persons who had come out under circumstances like my own, and who, on inquiry, had become convinced that they could effect nothing. He gave me a particular account of the three several contracts formed with the Mexican government by Zavala, Vehlein, and Burnet, for whom the Company professed to act as agents in trust; and though he made a clear story, and seemed intimately acquainted with the whole subject, I flattered myself, that he might lie under some mistake, or at least that the result of the business would in some way or other be more favorable than it promised.

CHAPTER IV.

Two of my fellow passengers, who intended to visit Mr. McNeil's estate, kindly invited me to accompany them, a day or two after our arrival; and we set off together, one pleasant morning on foot, as we had but an excursion of ten miles to perform. The surface is level, and the forest was unbroken for most of the way, except by the path. Vines were abundant, which are said to bear plenty of fine grapes of different descriptions, chiefly red grapes. The general aspect of the woods was like that of our own in the Northern States; but the continued level had a singular appearance to my eye. The trees were live oak, red oak, peccan, wild peach, holly, cotton wood, &c. So far as I recollect, we passed but a single habitation on the way; but we saw many squirrels, hogs, and deer, in different places in the forest, and several times tried our skill in shooting at them: for we had taken our guns with us.

I never shall forget my feelings at the sight of an

object I saw near the banks of the Brazos.   Through the misty morning air, a singular sight was presented to my view, among the trees of the forest.   There stood before me a mass of vegetation, the greater part of which appeared dead, and dry, and pendant in streamers from numerous points, ready to be waved by the wind whenever it should blow.   The form was ill defined, but the solid parts by which this loose outer drapery must have been supported, was concealed, though here and there large and knarled branches and tufts of deep verdure were dimly perceptible, through an almost unbroken veil of white and matted moss.   After admiring and wondering for a time, and approaching a little nearer, I perceived that this singular appearance was caused by a full grown tree of considerable age, with trunk and boughs which seemed as firm as iron, and laden with luxuriant foliage of a peculiar depth and darkness, overspread with lichens, hanging in bunches from the extremity of every branch, and twig, and concealing almost entirely the form, frame-work, and dark verdure beneath.   When the light fell upon it strongly, the whiteness of the moss, contrasted with the dark hue of the leaves, made it seem almost as pure as a hill of snow, and offered a striking resemblance to the hoary head of a venerable old patriarch.   The same kind of feeling, of mingled awe and love, were excited by the view: and I could hardly have persuaded myself, without the experience,

3*

that any object in the vegetable world could have produced an effect on my mind so much like that excited, under ordinary circumstances, by the presence of a dignified human being. I was gratified when I learned that this noble tree was a live oak, and that this product of the forest, so proverbial for the strength and durability of its timber, and so useful in the construction of ships, is generally distinguishable from a distance by being more fully arrayed than other trees in this singular drapery. I saw others as we proceeded, and found them all well shaped for strength, that is with rather angular or crooked branches, and with few marks of decay, or extreme age. The bark is generally smooth, and the whole aspect of the live oak is that of a tree designed of a firm and enduring manhood.

We were now in the midst of the district in which the live oak is found. It extends along the coast between Galveston and Matagorda Bays, and, it is said, about seventy miles into the interior. I saw none here of very great size : but near Bolivar are two, one of sixteen, the other nineteen feet girth ; and it is common, in some parts, to meet with large trees of this species, especially where they grow alone, or less crowded by others.

The fine estate which we were to visit, presented a beautiful appearance as we approached it. Before us spread an almost boundless plain, or natural meadow, a large part of which, owned by Mr. Mc-

Neil, is appropriated to grazing, and left unenclosed, with the exception of a single tract, as a vast pasture ground for his cattle. The enclosure, though it seemed to bear a small proportion to the whole estate, embraces not less than two hundred acres, and is secured from the encroachment of the cattle by a substantial fence of twelve rails.

It contains the garden, with a noble cotton field, which, the year before, had yielded a crop that sold for five thousand dollars. Even after it had been removed, one of our companions, who was from Alabama, declared there was still as good a crop then on the ground as they commonly gathered in his own state.

We directed our course towards his dwelling, which is a good log house, just on the verge of a fine grove, partly shaded by China trees, newly planted before it for ornament, and overlooking his whole domain.

We were received with great hospitality by Mr. McNeil and his family, in which we found every disposition to welcome us. They set before us the best products of the soil, which is indeed a land flowing with milk and honey, in a more unqualified sense of the expression than any I had ever seen. Our exercise had sharpened our appetites; and we were soon cheered with the sight of an excellent and plentiful meal: for our hosts, without making a single allusion to the subject, had immediately given

directions, on our first arrival, that our wants should
be provided for, and we soon sat down to a well
timed repast. It consisted chiefly of venison and a
fine turkey, and was accompanied with excellent
coffee. The daughter of our host was a very intelligent and well educated young lady, and had recently
returned from the Northern States, where she had
just completed her education.

After eating, we took a view of the charming scene
around us. The house in which we were, constructed
of logs, and on the plan common to the country
dwellings of farmers in Texas, is well sheltered from
the sun and the winds by the wood, in the verge of
which it is situated ; and when the beautiful China
trees around it shall have attained a greater size, the
spot will be rendered still more agreeable. The
mansion fronts upon the estate : a fine, open Prairie
over which the eye ranges with pleasure, no wild or
barren spot occurring to interrupt the universal aspect
of fertility and beauty, and no swelling of the surface
being perceptible, which might in any degree interfere
with the clearest view of every part. The only
interruption is caused by clusters of trees of different
forms and sizes, scattered at distant intervals here
and there. These clumps and groves, apparently
possessing all the neatness and beauty which could
have been given them if planted by the hand of man,
and tended by his greatest care, added the charm of
variety to the eye, while they promised thick and

convenient shelter from sun and storm to man or beast. Without such variety and such a refuge, the aspect of the Prairie, with all its verdure, would have been monotonous to the sight, and disheartening to the traveller. It would be almost impossible for a person who has never seen them, to imagine the appearances of these groves. Although they are wholly the work of nature, they often present all the beauty of art : for the trees are of nearly equal size, and grow near together, without underwood, and present outlines perfectly well defined, and often surprisingly regular. Some appear to form exact circles or ovals, while others are nearly square or oblong. It is no uncommon thing to see a continued line, running perfectly strait, for a mile or more in length, with scarcely a single tree projecting beyond it : so that I found it difficult to divest myself of the impression, that much of the land had been lately cleared, and that these were but the remains of the forest.

These groves are called islands, from the striking resemblance they present to small tracts of land surrounded by water. Nothing can be more natural, than the comparison. The Prairie assumes the uniform appearance of a lake, both in surface and color ; and in the remoter parts the hue melts into that of distant water ; and it requires no very great effort of the imagination, especially in certain states

of the weather and changes of the light, to fancy
that such is the nature of the scene.

The landscape was bounded on the right by a long
and distant line of woodland, which concealed and
yet betrayed the course of the river San Bernard,
and about three miles off, and on the left by a similar
limit, which formed the "bottoms" of the Brazos.
Between these the Prairie extended its broad, unbroken level before us about ten miles, beyond which
we saw the Gulf of Mexico, reaching off to the
horizon.

I stood long contemplating this charming picture,
which, as I before remarked, is entirely overlooked
from the door of our hospitable friend; and what
greatly added to its interest, was a vast number of
cattle feeding in all parts of his wide domain.　How
different a sight was here presented, from any of the
rural scenes with which my eyes had ever before
been familiar! How different was all the system of
the farmer from that prevailing in those regions of
my own country which I had lately visited! I was
one moment struck with surprise at the vast extent
of land under the care of a single proprietor, and the
few human hands required to perform the necessary
labor; and the next I was filled with admiration at
the various advantages afforded by a mild and
benignant climate, a soil of extreme fertility, and a
surface best appropriate to its use, when subjected to

a system of culture to which it was best adapted.
The cotton field and garden, with their two hundred
acres, lay on the one hand, effectually secured
against all encroachment with the most substantial
fence I had ever seen, which stretched off a mile on
one line; and around and beyond it lay the almost
boundless Prairie, variegated with its numerous
islands, spotted with a scattered herd of six hundred
cattle, all belonging to our host. The breed is larger
than those common in the north, with longer and
straiter limbs, broader horns and smoother coats.
They all appeared well fed, active and vigorous, and
spend their lives through winter and summer, in the
open air. The only attention bestowed upon them,
is merely to mark them when young in such a
manner that if they stray they may be distinguished
from the cattle of any other proprietor. Of course
no housing is necessary in such a climate, and no
provision of food for them is to be made, in a country
where there is perpetual green. They feed during
the winter in the bottoms, and as yet do not require
salt, for some reason unaccountable to me. One
might expect that cattle left thus to herd together in
such immense droves, without the care or control
of man during their lives, would contract habits of
timidity or of fierceness; but I was assured that
they are in one respect more manageable than the
tame cattle I have seen: for a horseman can

always readily separate such as he chooses from a
herd, by riding after them one at a time, though
this is a task of great difficulty with our northern
cattle, even where they have roads and fences to
restrain them.

CHAPTER V.

An Indian hunter shooting a deer on the Prairie.—Visit to Mr. Westall's estate.—Hospitality naturally resulting from such a mode of life.—A well.—Singular excitement among a large herd of cattle.—A wolf.—A bee tree.—Return to Brazoria.

WHILE we were looking at the fine scene before us, and hearing of the habits of the wild deer, which often come to feed among the oxen, Mr. McNeil discovered one at the distance of a mile, and directed that his huntsman should be sent to shoot it, supposing that we might wish to see the execution of a task which at least one of our party had lately began to regard as not a very simple one. The hunter made his appearance, and prepared to perform his duty. He was a short, copper-colored, strait-haired man, in a tight buff deer skin dress, mounted on a fiery little horse, and armed with a rifle, being the first Indian I had seen since entering Texas. We were informed that he is kept by Mr. McNeil for the sole purpose of supplying the family with game; and this he furnishes in such quantities, that a large share of all the food eaten is of his procuring. To him we had already been indebted for the fine dish of venison on which we had dined. At the

4

command of his master he set off at a quick rate, towards the spot where the deer was grazing in apparent security, among a number of cattle, but by such a direction as to get to the windward. As he proceeded rapidly along the Prairie his size seemed to diminish, but we kept him in view, occasionally casting an eye at the object of his mission, which appeared like a very small animal from the distance at which we stood : probably about three miles. As the hunter came nearer, and when there was some risk of his being observed by the deer, he dismounted, placed himself on the side of his horse, opposite that which was towards the object of his pursuit, made him proceed in the same direction, keeping cautiously on the watch. Thus he gradually stole on, until he was within fair shot of his mark : then pointing his piece, the smoke rose, and the deer fell, and in a moment more he had it thrown across his horse, and was returning rapidly towards us with his prize.

There was abundance of snipe near the house, but I was ridiculed for thinking of such insignificant game.

Having thus, in a short time, seen much to gratify me on this beautiful estate, I set off in the afternoon with one of my companions, to visit the family of Mr. Westall, a neighboring planter, to whom he had a letter of introduction. His house, which stands at the distance of a mile, was in sight from Mr. Mc-

Neil's; and on reaching it it proved to be situated in a similar manner, handsomely shaded by the outer trees of an island, and yet commanding an uninterrupted view out upon an extensive tract of Prairie, with a herd of six or seven hundred fine cattle. In one respect the house had the advantage over any other country residence I recollect to have seen in Texas: it was surrounded with a handsome yard, neatly fenced in; and planted with rows of the China tree. We were received with hospitality, and spent our time in pleasant conversation with Mr. Westall and his family, who were interested in almost every thing we could speak of relating to the United States. Such curiosity as we usually found during our travels, is the very natural result of meeting intelligent minds secluded from intercourse with the world. Our companion who remained at Mr. Mc-Neil's afterwards informed me, that he set up a great part of the night conversing with his host. Every well behaved stranger, on account of the news he brings, is a welcome visitor in such families as these; and this fact, in connexion with the general prosperity of the people, and the kind dispositions of a large portion of them, renders their hospitality very sincere. To be received at the house of strangers with cheerfulness and pleasure, and welcomed with every favor in their power, is doubly agreeable when you feel that your society is regarded as a rich reward for all you receive; and this we often found to be the case when we engaged in cheerful conversation, and readily imparted what information we possessed on subjects interesting to those about us.

Mr. Westall, in connexion with two or three other persons, a few years since, purchased a large tract of land here for three dollars an acre. Mr. McNeil obtained a square league through Mr. Austin, as an " empresario."

We found the water on this estate remarkably good, which we regarded as a great luxury, as we had before found only such as was indifferent or unpalatable. Mr. Westall informed us, that it came from a well in which he had succeeded in obtaining a fine spring, after several unavailing attempts in different places near his house. He took us to the spot, which was in the midst of a grass plat. He had remarked that the verdure was deeper in that place than elsewhere, and suspecting that this might be owing to a supply of moisture from below, sunk a well, and obtained what he sought. Stones are not to be found in all this region, and we learnt that the sides of the well were planked, as a substitute for stoning. This is the common resort through the country, wherever wells are used, which is very rare.

We found much to admire in Mr. Westall's system of farming. Every thing seemed well planned, and well executed. Order and neatness, as well as intelligent arrangements, success and prosperity, appeared on all sides.

The cattle, scattered over the spacious plain before us, were feeding, or lying down or straying about as they pleased; and, though the scene was less extensive which we overlooked from this house than from that we had left, as it did not reach to the Gulf, it was scarcely inferior in beauty in other respects. It would be difficult to imagine a landscape more expressive of tranquillity and repose. The most distant cattle were apparently reduced to so small a size, that one could not have distinguished them from much smaller animals had they been alone. Now it was easy to realize that the numerous spots on the Prairie, one two and three miles distant, were large, sleek and vigorous cattle like those near us, and belonged to the same great herd to which that vast pasture ground was appropriated.

But a sudden accident changed the whole aspect of this tranquil scene. A bellowing was heard on the verge of a wood, which caused the cattle to raise their heads and listen, and soon began to attract them towards the spot. Those at a distance soon left feeding and proceeded thither also—not at a slow and leisurely gait—but with a rapid motion, a wild and angry look, and occasionally with a loud bellowing in return. To me the scene was entirely new, and I was quite at a loss to account for it. All hurried with one consent towards one point, evidently influenced by similar and violent feelings, nor did they give over their race nor slacken their speed until they reached the place. Some of them we could see starting from a distance of two, and I presume even three miles, and steering in a direct line across the Prairie. Others were arriving every moment from different quarters, until the number assembled was so great, that it was much easier than before to realize the size of this noble herd. The cause of this muster was explained, when we were informed that a wolf had seized a calf on the borders of the wood, whose cries had called all the cattle to its succor. This is an affair of frequent occurrence, as I was assured. The herd are always ready to repel such an assailant; and I am sure would have been sufficient to overwhelm a far more powerful enemy, excited as they were, and ready to rush in a mass, as they seemed to be, on any opponent.

The people represent it as dangerous to venture among cattle while thus enraged; and we did not approach the spot until the following day, when, however, we were unable to discover any traces of the wolf or his prey, and therefore presumed that the former had fled and the latter had escaped without fatal injury.

In the morning, which was not less clear and pleasant than the preceding, we set off on our return, after an excellent nights' rest, calling at Mr. McNeil's on our way, to take our companion with us. We lounged through the woods at our leisure, shooting squirrels, and occasionally straying from the path as far as we dare, in pursuit of game, but never venturing to lose sight of each other, for fear of getting bewildered in the level forest. We remarked that the road often deviated considerably from a strait line: indeed it is so crooked that the shortest distance between its two extremities is only six miles, while the actual route measures ten. The bends were made in opening the road, to avoid cane brakes, and those parts of the forest where the timber was too thick to be easily cut through.

Near the house of Mr. McNeil we saw in the woods a "Bee tree." Wild honey is very abundant in this country, and is obtained at the expense of only a little care and labor, from the hollow trees in which it is deposited. About twenty feet from the ground was a hole, in and out of which the bees were continually flying; and there was every probability that a large store was laid up within, but we passed on, and left the industrious insects in possession of their treasure.

CHAPTER VI.

On my return to Brazoria I found two gentlemen had arrived from San Felipe during our absence, and, with a wish to obtain all possible information concerning the nature of the land I had purchased, and particularly the title which I held, I sought them out. I was gratified to find that one of them was a gentleman to whom I had a letter of intro-duction, and from whom I had expected to derive the information I desired on arriving at San Felipe, whither I had designed to proceed, as I knew he had been there to make inquiries for himself, being interested like me in a purchase of the Galveston Bay and Texas Land Company. I soon ascertained from him that my worst fears were too well founded, and that my hopes were all fallacious. He had already renounced his own expectations, and lament-ed his disappointments.

I had now some painful and mortifying reflections to make after the receipt of the information I had obtained in relation to the principal object of my voyage. I found that my confidence in the names of a few respectable individuals appended to the advertisements of a company, had betrayed me into much disappointment, as well as some pecuniary loss. Although I could not doubt that men of honesty, on learning the state of the case, would be forward to repay me the money which I now saw I had paid them for nothing, I could not look for an adequate remuneration for my travelling expenses, my time, or the interruption of my business.

On an examination of the subject, with the facts now before me, I found such was the situation of things, that I derived no advantage whatever from the payment of money I had made, having not a foot of land, nor any claim to offer superior to that of any other man who might come into Texas from a foreign country. I might easily obtain a quarter of a league of unappropriated land, on condition of professing the Roman Catholic religion, becoming a citizen of the Republic of Mexico, and residing on the soil for six years, receiving the title from the government; but not otherwise; and this was a standing offer to any person who might choose to accept of it. In case of marriage, either before or after the contract, the amount was to be quadrupled. The government had never conferred on any individual or company the title to any extensive tract of land, or authority to stipulate for any thing beyond, or contrary to these conditions.

Maps of Texas published in the United States indeed represent the territory as almost covered with what are generally denominated Grants or Colonies: but they are neither one nor the other in the common meaning of the terms. I had been extremely misled on this important subject.

The Mexican Congress in 1824, passed a general law to encourage emigration, which they recommended as the basis of laws to be passed by the several states. The object of the plan was, to admit Roman Catholics of good character willing to become citizens of the country, but to exclude others. Such laws were passed by the States, and, among others, by that of Coahuila and Texas. Under this system the agency of contractors was engaged, who are called empresarios, or undertakers. To them were assigned the tracts improperly called grants or colonies, into which they were to introduce certain numbers of settlers on specified terms. These were generally as follows : that if the assigned number were introduced, of the character and description required by law, within a specified term of a few years, and became permanent settlers, without expense to the government, the empresarios should receive five square leagues of land for every hundred families introduced. The settlers, after proving their "religious" character, as it is called, (that is, furnishing evidence that they are Roman Catholics,) and after signing their contracts, &c, according to law, and paying certain charges, were to receive from the government a clear title : a single man to a quarter of a square league, and a married man to a whole square league.

Thus the settler had not to purchase a title of the agent or empresario, nor was the latter authorized or enabled to confer upon the settler, either for money or for nothing, any advantage or benefit whatever, beyond those offered by the government, as just stated, to any applicants who would comply with the fixed conditions. It might be more convenient for strangers to obtain information through agents or empresarios; but they were not expected to obtain them under more or less favorable terms than if they made direct application to the state government through the proper authority. Settlers were not in fact, prevented from applying to which they might choose : for even in the tracts marked off on the maps to different individuals, the government exercise the right of settling as many as they please, and in terms claim the surplus after the stipulated number of settlers shall have been located, and the empresarios remunerated with their tracts. In some of them are also comprehended tracts conferred upon officers of the army, generally eleven miles square, and with titles vested, though they are still for the most part unoccupied.

Now, through ignorance of these circumstances I had been led into a foolish bargain, from which a

plain statement like that I have here made would
have saved me, if it had been made in season. Had
the facts been distinctly published in the United States,
they would also have prevented many occurrences,
much more to be regretted than the mere loss of time
and money which I had suffered.   This statement
I have now here brought before the public : so that
if any one hereafter makes a wild goose chase of
the kind, he may not, like me, be able to plead entire
ignorance of the case.

It is natural enough that a person in the United
States, on seeing fertile land advertised *for sale*, with
many recommendations of the situation, climate,
&c., to presume that money paid to the advertiser
will purchase some title to it.   And when the names
of responsible men are given as those concerned in
the business, that there is a reasonable guarantee for
good faith.   But what would the active managers of
the concerns of the Galveston Bay and Texas Land
Company have said ; what would the respectable
gentlemen of New-York, whose names were among
its officers have felt, if they had been among those
persons who had gone to that distant territory under
the inducements thus held out, after investing their
money in the scrip, and witnessed their disappointment?

When I ascertained the facts in the case, I could
not think of myself alone : I knew that numbers
had already come out to Texas under impressions

as erroneous as my own : and supposed that many more were on the way. I believed too that the company were still selling scrip, and that probably hundreds of persons, families and all, had by this time embarked in the same incautious speculation. The more I reflected, the more strange it appeared, that men could be induced to proceed in so blindfold a manner : but I thought the truth must certainly soon become known, and put a stop to such proceedings.

However, my own course was very plain, as it appeared to me after the first feelings of disappointment and vexation had passed. I was in Texas, and could not immediately get out of it. I must wait some time for an opportunity to return to the United States; the country, as far as I could judge, had hardly been overrated for fertility and beauty; and I might spend some weeks agreeably and with improvement in making observations.

Among the settlements in the country, which are still few and small, one of the most recent was Anahuac, on Galveston Bay. As yet it was a mere village, with a military post of no considerable importance : but there a few emigrants, (brought out by the Galveston Bay and Texas Land Company,) had been landed, and more might soon be expected. It was perfectly plain that those strangers must find themselves in a very unpleasant situation. What they were to do I did not know ; for on landing in the country they must have learnt with surprise and disappointment, the same facts which had given me so much pain; and, being generally poor, would have no means to return to the United States. There was one course which they might pursue. They might take land from the State Government, through Mr. Austin, or the Mexican authorities: but they were not provided with implements, stock, &c., and how could they cultivate the soil, or in any manner support themselves?

My two new friends intended to proceed immediately thither; and I concluded to accompany them, as there would be the most probable point for the early reception of news from the United States: several vessels with emigrants being understood to be on the passage.

The first thing to be attended to, was the purchase of a horse; and this was easy to be effected. The small horses of the country, called *mustangs*, introduced by the Spaniards, and now numerous in the more northern prairies, run wild in droves over these parts of Texas, and are easily taken and rendered serviceable by the inhabitants. When caught, it would be a problem to a stranger to confine them, where there is neither tree nor rock to be found: but the Mexicans put on a halter, knot it at the end, dig a hole about ten inches deep, put in the knot, and press the earth down upon it. The pull being sideways is at a disadvantage, and the horse is unable to draw it out. They are driven to market, purchased for three or four dollars, branded, hobbled, turned out again, and entirely abandoned to themselves until they are needed. Whenever a vessel arrives, some of the inhabitants send into the woods and cane brakes for such a number as they suppose may be wanted by the passengers; and this I found had already been done, in anticipation of the wants of those who came in the sloop Majesty. In the log stable belonging to Mr. Austin, at whose house I lodged, I saw a number of them, with all the wild look which might be expected from their habits of life. They are small, generally about 13 hands high, well formed, rather for strength, and of different colors. I saw others in several other stables; and at length made choice of a white one; and having paid for him a doubloon and four dollars, (a handsome advance on his original cost,) stuffed a pair of saddle bags with a few articles of food as well as clothes, and was soon ready for my journey.

As the brands on horses afford the only evidence of their identity, and the property of their owners, the rules observed in respect to them are very strict.

These horses are very useful in the country, and may perhaps become at some future time a valuable article of export, as they are innumerable, and cost only the trouble of catching. This is done with a strong noosed cord, made of twisted strips of raw hide, and called a *lazo*, which is the Spanish word for a band or bond. It has been often described, as well as the manner of throwing it, as it is in common use for catching animals, and sometimes for choking men, in different parts of America inhabited by the descendants of the Spanish and Portugese. A man on horseback, with a rope of this kind coiled in his left hand, and one end of it fastened to the horse, whirls the noosed end in the air over his head as he approaches the animal he intends to seize : and, on finding an opportunity, throws it over its head or horns, and checks his horse. The noose is instantly drawn tight, and the poor creature is thrown violently down, without the power of moving, and generally deprived of breath. They are sometimes badly injured, and even killed, by being dashed to the ground ; but generally escape with a severe practical lesson on the nature of this rude instrument of civilization, which they afterwards hold in great respect all their lives, yielding immediately whenever they feel it again upon their necks.

The mustangs often carry to their graves evidence of the violent means adopted by the Mexicans in breaking them to the bridle. Many of them are foundered, or otherwise diseased. A horse which has been lazoed is blindfolded, mounted by a rider armed with the heavy and barbarous spurs of the country, after having their terrible lever bits put into his mouth, a moderate pull upon which might break his jaw ; and if he runs is pricked to his speed, till

he falls down with exhaustion. He is then turned in the opposite direction, and cruelly spurred again. If he is found able to run back to the point from which he started, he is thought to have bottom enough to make a valuable horse : otherwise he is turned off as good for little or nothing. The process is a brutal one ; and the agony inflicted by the bits is extreme : as blood flows freely from the mouth which is often greatly swollen ; and the animal yields to mere force.

In the morning we mounted our horses and proceeded to the river, where the ferry boat, a large scow, was lying near the shore. I dismounted, and taking the bridle in my hand, attempted to lead my horse in after me. Most fortunately I was looking at him, and was better prepared than I was sensible of being, to make one of those sudden instinctive motions, which sometimes prove essential to our safety. Had I been turning the other way, or a little less active, I should probably have lost my life, or at least have been seriously injured : for instead of following me into the boat, as an honest horse should, and as I had expected him to do, he fixed his eyes upon me with a malicious expression, and sprung at me like lightning, clearing the ground entirely, and making a leap of about eight feet. I jumped aside, and barely in time to avoid his feet, with which it seemed to me he designed to beat me down. I do not know that I ever had experienced such feelings

as this occurrence excited in me. It betrayed a
degree of spite mingled with craft which I had never
seen in an animal of his species; and laid the axe
at the root of all that confidence and attachment
which a traveller loves to exercise towards his horse.
I have been thus particular in mentioning this little
occurrence, because the wit of the country appears
to be largely invested in the horses; and this was
the beginning of my white mustang.

CHAPTER VII.

THE first three or four miles of our way lay through woods, in the bottom land, after which we entered a Prairie, where we found the house of Mr. Bailey, situated seven miles from Brazoria. It is a wooden house; and, being painted red, presented a very novel appearance for Texas. When we dismounted, I tied my horse to a small tree with his halter, and accompanied my companions into the house. The proprietor approached to welcome us with the usual salutation, which often afterwards sounded so hospitable in my ears at the close of a fatiguing ride: "Walk in, stranger." But he was so lame that he could hardly walk, and so hoarse that it was with difficulty he could make himself understood. These, he told us, were effects of an accident with a vicious horse. He had purchased a mustang a few days before for twenty dollars, which threw him violently over his head, and was near breaking his bones. The concussion was so severe, that he was not likely to recover from it in a long time; and he still felt so much irritated, that he told us in an animated manner how he had immediately butchered the offending animal, by cutting his throat, being determined that he should never expose another rider to such danger. He pronounced those poor little animals to be the most perverse, treacherous and trickish creatures in the world, and destitute of all the generous traits of character which are found in the common horse. Much of this I was disposed to attribute to his resentment against the beast he had put to death: for how, thought I, can the mustang of Texas be so different from his brethren of other countries?

From Mr. Bailey's house we enjoyed another charming Prairie scene. He had fifty or sixty acres under cultivation; and there was a similar extensive and fertile plain, varied with many verdant "islands," endlessly diversified in form, size and relative position, on which not a trace was to be seen of the fire which had passed over it in the winter, and which must have blackened the surface and deformed the landscape until spring had brought up the fresh grass to clothe it in a new robe of green. The cattle, which were feeding on the plain, had sought shelter in the beautiful and isolated groves; for the heat of the sun was already powerful at mid-day; the thermometer ranging that day as follows, as I afterwards learnt at Anahuac: morning, 64° noon, 66° night, 60°.

It was our intention to proceed to Bingham's that day : for one of my companions, who had travelled the road a short time before, had calculated that his house would afford us a very comfortable lodging after a good day's ride. We rose therefore to proceed on our journey. But I had a chapter or two more to read on the character of mustangs before I was destined to leave the place. I had never been informed of one particular propensity which they have, that is, to draw back and pull violently when approached in front, and therefore walked up to my white horse rather hastily to untie and mount him. He sprang back and pulled for a moment so hard upon the sapling to which I had fastened him, that it came up by the roots ; and after a few leaps and kicks, which freed him from my saddle bags, and broke the bridle, he made off towards the middle of the Prairie at full speed, with his head and tail both raised, and in a state of exultation which formed quite a contrast to my own feelings.

My companions threw off their valises, mounted immediately, and gave chase to the pestilent runaway, which, after a short gallop, had halted, and with the most provoking coolness began to eat grass from the Prairie. As they approached him, however, he flew off again as fast as his legs would carry him ; and thus he led them to a great distance, on a chase apparently hopeless. I watched them till I was tired, coursing over the Prairie here and there, now

on this side, now on that, at such a distance that
they looked no bigger than cats, and anon further
diminished to mere mice. My white mustang led
them up and down, round and crosswise, as if he
delighted in worrying them, occasionally stopping,
as coolly as before, to crop the grass, and then off in
a new direction, like a wild creature as he was.
This chase lasted without intermission for four
hours, at the end of which they succeeded in
driving the little white animal towards the house.
Mr. Bailey, seeing him approaching, despatched a
messenger to a neighboring farm for assistance; and
a man soon came hurrying down on horseback,
provided with a lazo: a rope with a noose at the
end as before described. He joined in the pursuit
with the spirit and skill of one practised in such an
employment, and soon got within about eight or ten
feet of my horse, when, with a dexterous fling, he
suddenly threw the noose over his head. Having
the beast now completely in his power, he was prepared to choke him into submission; and the noose
was on the point of closing its grasp round his neck.
But here the intelligence and experience of the
mustang stepped in with customary promptitude:
for as soon as he felt the rope round his neck, he
stopped stone still, and yielded as submissively as a
lamb. Like an accomplished rogue at last fairly in
the gripe of justice, he seemed in haste to submit,
plead guilty and repent, in order to secure as much

leniency as possible; and in a few moments I was
again on the back of this little flying brute, jogging
on as quietly as if he had never rebelled in his life.
There was a great deal of farce in all this: but we
had been put to too much inconvenience by the
perverse trick to enjoy the joke: for our loss of time,
we foresaw, would put it out of our power to perform
all our intended day's journey.

It was nearly dark when we reached Hall's: a
habitation of which I had heard, but at which we
had not originally intended to stop, as it was only
thirteen miles from Bailey's. I here found that
horses in Texas are always turned out loose to feed,
even if a traveller stops but for the night, which
would have ensured another chase, with perhaps
even more unfavorable results than that I had witnessed, but for an expedient which was recommended
to us. This was to "hobble them" after the fashion
of the country: which consists in tying together
their fore legs with a short cord, and not one fore
and one hind leg together, as we do at the north.
This operation instantly changes the movements of
a horse, as he is obliged to make every step a fair
leap; and it excited the greatest merriment in me,
when I saw the horses of my companions practising
a gait so different from common, under a mode of
constraint which I had never witnessed before. Fully
satisfied that such confinement would be sufficient

even for my white mustang, I began to tie his legs together, which to my surprise he submitted to with the utmost cheerfulness, without raising his head, for he had already began to graze on the fine grass. Although so recently accustomed to run at large in the Brazos forests, he had evidently been familiar with the hobble: for as if he perfectly concurred in my opinion as to the propriety of his being bound, whenever he wanted to move he carefully raised both fore feet together, so as not to interfere with my task, and made a gentle spring to a knot of fresh feed. Surely, thought I, I have got a steed sagacious enough to figure in one of Æsop's Fables.

In the morning we enjoyed the sight of a large enclosure around the house, filled with young orange and fig trees, as well as many other kinds of fruit, which, in the early and sloping light, offered a rich and varied sight.

We were on the road early, and went on to Mr. Bingham's to breakfast. This house was ornamented with young China trees, and the best I had seen in the country, though built of logs, on the common plan, and only of one story, as the logs were fitted with great care, planed off, and partly lined with smooth boards; the owner having a saw mill near, then the only one in this part of the country. The want of more was severely felt in every part of Texas, and offered the greatest encouragement for the erection of mills.

Here, as at the other houses which I had thus far seen, we were received with every mark of plain hospitality. The negroes, (here, as on most other estates, real slaves, though nominally "bound" for ever,) were called to take care of our horses, though I preferred to perform that task for myself, as I trusted I should be able to attach my own to me by offices of kindness. The negroes waited on us at table, where, according to custom, the lady of the house presided; and we had a variety of good food placed before us, all the products of the soil except the coffee, which was remarkably fine.

I conversed with our host on his manner of cultivation. He thinks his slaves indispensable: but I am convinced that white men would prove more profitable laborers, even in raising cotton. The past winter was considered the hardest ever known throughout the south western country, and the season was backward, so that the cotton was just coming out of the ground.

Mr. Bingham has about six hundred cattle. We passed through the herd as they were feeding on the Prairie, and they looked wild, but we were informed that they were on the contrary quite tame and tractable, considering their free habits. The proprietor is the most influential man in the vicinity for some miles, and lives in the best manner of a Texas farmer, with abundance around him, and a system of management successfully carried out on his

estate. In the domestic branch, every thing spoke
industry and order. His wife, a lady of much
intelligence and good breeding, acknowledged that
a change of residence to Texas had cost her a great
struggle, but declared that she has since become
quite reconciled to her abode, and does not feel that
want of society which she apprehended. She has
four or five children, and several neighbors around
her, and can at any time, as she remarked, pay a
visit to a friend by taking a short ride of ten or
twenty miles.

It was surprising to see in how short a time a
settler, with a moderate sum of money in hand,
could become independent in such a country. Mr.
Bingham had been here only three or four years,
and, in addition to the other advantages I have
mentioned, his house was supplied with the best
furniture I any where met with in Texas.
This he had brought from the United States, to
which he had generally made a journey annually.
One great advantage enjoyed here over some new
countries, is found in the superior healthiness of the
climate, of which I heard uniform testimony from
all with whom I conversed, confirmed by the robust
and cheerful aspect of the inhabitants.

We learnt that Oyster Bayou lay near us; but,
being in the forest, (or, as it is commonly expressed
there, "in the timber,") we did not see it from the
house. Oysters are taken from it, of good quality,

and in considerable quantity. I took a walk through the timber, to fish in the Bayou, but caught only a few from the shore, though they are abundant at certain seasons. They have one species which they call trout, but it is quite unlike our own. On the opposite bank of the Bayou was Mr. Bingham's field, or cultivated ground. It contains two hundred acres, and is pretty well secured against the encroachments of cattle by its situation, being nearly surrounded by water. I was informed, however, that they sometimes swim across and enter it. The corn was about six inches high, very green and spread over a space of one hundred acres, uninterrupted by a fence or other obstruction. He had also some acres planted with cotton. The soil of this tract was that of a cane brake, which he had cleared, and which passes for the best kind of land, especially when the wild peach tree is found growing upon it, when it is called peach and cane land.

CHAPTER VIII.

WE took our departure for Harrisburgh, by a road which had been but little travelled, and found the way much impeded by the late rains. This proved to be more particularly the case during the latter part of our ride. Road, there was none: we travelled by the compass. Half of our route lay over level ground, and half over a rolling country.

We came to a bayou, about fifty feet wide, which lay before us, and one of my companions rode in, but found the mud so deep, and met so much difficulty in getting over, that he had to swim his horse. We therefore rode farther on in search of a more convenient spot. My other companion next made an experiment, and got over also, but in a place which proved worse than the former; and after passing still farther on, I was obliged also to try the experiment, but did not reach the opposite bank until I had heartily repented my not following the first example. My horse, which had long been drooping, soon after this began to lose his courage as well as to slacken his pace, being wearied, as I supposed, by the labor of travelling on a very bad road, now perceptibly growing worse. The mud was so deep, that our animals sunk in three or four inches at every step. We deviated from the road to seek better ground, and at length lost it entirely. Our prospects thus became more and more gloomy the farther we proceeded.

A tired horse in such circumstances was peculiarly forbidding even in the idea; but something worse than mere apprehension soon succeeded. We observed a cart at a distance, and proceeded to it to inquire our way of the owner, when at a moment when I was not prepared against accidents, my white mustang fell to the ground, and threw me over his head into the mud. I feared he might seize the opportunity and give me the slip; but on observing him, there seemed to be little danger of his ever running away again. He had the most perfect appearance of being overdone, and I began to fear it would be impossible to get him to Harrisburgh. It was true the distance we had come was not great, nor was the road, which was generally level, so extremely bad as I had sometimes travelled: but to an animal of his size, and unaccustomed to labor as I supposed he had long been before he was caught for my use, perhaps a little fatigue might have proved unequal to his strength. His pitiable plight filled me with compassion as well as concern; and, relieving him of my saddle bags, which one of my companions kindly offered to take, I took the bridle, and began to lead him slowly on, being convinced that he was quite unable to carry me any further. The remainder of the way to Harrisburgh was not a whit better, though we had a wide space to choose our route from; but I walked the whole distance, followed by my poor, worn out mustang, and was rejoiced when I found him safe in the village, after a journey of thirty miles, as I had many apprehensions on the way that he would never be able to reach it.

The surface around Harrisburgh is of that kind which is called a "rolling country:" that is, it lies in gradual swells of moderate elevation, which present a constant variety of scenes, as the traveller changes his point of view at almost every step. The land was not very good, but the corn fields in some places looked very well. The forests are composed of pine and oak trees, the latter of which may be compared with that of the northern states for quality, but the pine is inferior. At this place was the only steam saw mill at that time in the country. The engine works also a flour mill, where one fifth is taken for toll. It was found very profitable, although not worked with proper attention to economy, as the lumber is admitted into all the Mexican ports without

duty, while from the United States it was almost
excluded. They did not heat the boilers until after
breakfast, and emptied them daily at sun set. The
price of boards was forty dollars a thousand. The
mill is on Buffalo Bayou, about thirty miles from
the Brazos river, and is accessible to vessels drawing
five or six feet of water The timber, yellow pine
and oak, is floated to the mills.

Three vessels were there on the 1st of April, waiting for loads of lumber for Tampico and Matamoras.
Mr. Harris told me he had orders for more than he
could supply. They might saw from three to five
thousand a day with proper industry.

The town had its name from Mr. Harris, the
owner of the mill. It contained only about twenty
houses, built almost entirely of logs, with only two
or three frame dwellings, and being laid out without
much regard to regularity. The house at which we
lodged, was very well kept. Though a log house,
our room was well furnished. The situation of the
village I judged to be rather unhealthy. We had
intended to proceed on our journey on the following
morning: but my horse appeared not to have gained
any thing by rest, refused to eat, and in spite of all
the coaxing and rubbing down I could give him,
seemed likely to die. Such an interruption was very
disagreeable; and I determined to procure another
animal. On inquiry, however, I found that was
impossible, as there were no horses for sale in the

place. Our party, therefore, spent half the day at Harrisburgh. After dinner I took another look at my horse, and could perceive no signs of improvement in his condition, so that I had a prospect of a much longer detention. After a little consideration, however, I determined to delay no longer, but make an experiment in travelling; for the mustang might as well die on the road as at pasture.

We took our departure accordingly; and I had much difficulty in getting my horse out of the town. In a short time, however, he began to cheer up, and gradually quickened his pace until his strength and spirits were quite restored, and he travelled remarkably well. However strange it may seem, there was every appearance that the whole affair had been a mere trick of the wily brute; and my opinion was confirmed by several inhabitants to whom I afterwards recounted the story. They told me that the sagacity and duplicity of the mustang is well known among them, and that he is capable of almost any thing, which ingenuity or malice can invent. So ungrateful a return for all my kindness and care, under such vexatious circumstances, and aggravated by such persevering imposture, added to my previous dislike of the animal which had been guilty of it.

We passed through a rolling country, principally open Prairie land, with numerous islands of wood seen in every direction, and crossed by many brooks and bayous.

On reaching one of the streams, finding it larger than usual, and seeing a woman washing clothes on the opposite shore, with a canoe, we requested her to bring it over to us, which she did. We had been joined by a stranger, so that we were four. We then took our saddles across with our horses, one at a time, by holding the bridle, sitting in the boat, and making them swim. With the three first we had no difficulty : but while attempting to lead the remaining one into the water, he unexpectedly leaped into the canoe, small and narrow as it was, and kept his balance so exactly as not to overset it. The impulse which he gave it, however, made it shoot out into the middle of the stream, so that my two companions who were in it, were half way over before they could recover from their surprise and consternation. The horse just then, by making a sudden turn of his head to look back at the land he had left, lost his balance and fell into the water, though in such a manner as not to turn the canoe over. He sunk, passed under it, rose on the opposite side, and swam to the shore, escaping with only a slight scratch on his leg. So extraordinary an occurrence, so ludicrous in itself, and attended by no unfortunate result, naturally caused the greatest merriment among us after all had safely reached the land.

We stopped for the night at Mr. Lynch's, on the western banks of the river San Jacinto, at the mouth of Buffalo Bayou. The land is very low and marshy, and the sallow countenances of the children indicate the unhealthiness of the situation. Mr. Lynch had a store, containing quite an assortment of goods, and was about erecting salt works on the opposite side of the river, where is good salt water. His house is an inn, and he keeps a ferry boat on the stream, for the convenience of travellers.

Mr. David S. Burnet, a new settler from New Jersey, was about to establish a steam saw mill at this place. It is said to be a very favorable position : there being large quantities of the finest timber on the banks of the stream, as I was informed. Pine, oak, and cedar logs may be cut, and floated down to the mill with great ease.

The next day we traversed a broad and beautiful prairie, where we could perceive no sign of a path, and where for miles there was not a tree to be seen unless at a great distance. Here are deer and wild horses, and the horns of stags often lie on the ground.

One of the prettiest little animals I ever saw, is the " horned frog;" which, notwithstanding its name, is far from being amphibious, as it is found on the prairies at a distance from water. Indeed it bears little or no resemblance to a frog, appearing more like a lizard, with rather a long and graceful form, a tail, and legs of nearly equal length, so that it runs swiftly and never leaps. I had often occasion to notice them, both here and on other prairies. They run with such agility, that although they do not take alarm until you have approached very near them, they dart off, and generally disappear immediately. One might often mistake them for quails, while in motion. They are of a yellowish color, mottled, and have horns about half an inch long, projecting from the front of the head. Several were caught and kept for some time in a barrel at Anahuac, and though it could not be perceived that they ate any of the various kinds of food which were offered them, they lived and continued active for a considerable time.

We crossed a stream by swimming, after a long ride; and our next halt was made at the house of Mr. Winfrey. He proposed to us to dine: but as we had determined to go a mile and a half further, to Barrow's, to dinner, we declined. One of the horses, however, which had not been properly secured, got off, and led us a long chase over the Prairie. I performed a more active part on this, than on a former occasion, when my own was the runaway; and we at length succeeded in our exertions, and found the table ready when we returned to the house. We spent the night there also. In the morning I was amused at the sight of one of our horses, which had been hobbled in the manner before described, but, on being found, had got his legs free, though he had not made the discovery. When his master began to drive him towards the house, he began to leap, as a hobbled animal must necessarily do, carefully raising both his fore feet together, and never attempting to take a step in any other manner. Seeing that he was perfectly free, we expected him soon to find it out: but he did not, and proceeded with this unnatural motion into the pen, near the house, a distance of half a mile. There he somehow or other came to the knowledge of the liberty of his limbs, and seemed very much astonished at the discovery; while we congratulated ourselves on having thus easily effected his imprisonment.

Mr. Barrow was engaged in a branch of business which has proved very profitable, and might be hereafter extensively pursued with success; that is, the raising of mules. Perhaps it may be considered one of the most lucrative, under proper management, which could be devised in Texas. Mules are almost exclusively used in the transportation of merchandise in Mexico by land, and large and numerous caravans are constantly moving in all parts of the republic. They thrive on coarse food, are hardy, and manageable in droves. This renders them valuable, and a good price may always be obtained for them. Good mules sell for from fifty to a hundred dollars apiece. Barrow had about seventy colts every season; and where grazing is so abundant, the expense of raising is very trifling. Very little use is made of oxen in Texas by the natives, in any kind of labor. They are said sometimes to employ them in the field, making them draw with the horns.

An American farmer emigrating to Texas should take out, as some do, a wagon ready to be driven into the country, wherever he might intend to settle. A set of such farming implements as he would use at home may be recommended, as I saw no reason to believe that any change would be advisable. He would then be prepared to move directly to his land, (unless indeed he had bought scrip of the Galveston Bay and Texas Land Company, whose land, as one of the Trustees told me on my return to New-York, "is not deliverable in Texas, but in Wall-street.") The oxen of the country are easily trained to the yoke, and, as may be supposed, may generally be purchased very low. Horses are seldom harnessed : such being at present the state of travelling. If then the settler is provided with the most necessary furniture, and provisions enough to live on, until he has time to get his subsistence from the soil and hunting, when he has built a log house he may consider himself as having made a fair beginning in life ; and with health, industry, and economy, can hardly fail of success.

7

CHAPTER IX.

Route from Brazoria to Anahuac continued.—A highway through the water.—Heyne's.—Vain attempt to overcome the scruples of a mustang.—Emigrants deserting.—Bottoms and timber.—Starting a deer, and starting ourselves.—Burning a cane brake.

Before leaving Barrow's, we made particular inquiries concerning the route we were to pursue to find our way to Anahuac. That place stands on the opposite side of a broad cove, forming the upper extremity of the great Bay of Galveston, a large part of which was in full view from the house. And now we learnt that we were to pursue a somewhat singular plan, to avoid a bayou which lay across our way in the most direct course. We were first to travel awhile over the Prairie, and then, taking to the water, wade our horses about a mile, at a considerable distance from the shore. Mr. Barrow assured us that the water was shallow, and the bottom very smooth, and that we need but to keep the proper direction and avoid mud holes, to find this way the most safe, agreeable, and expeditious. Indeed the difficulty of passing the bayou, with its deep channel and steep banks, was such as to put that task almost out of the question.

After proceeding, therefore, about as far as we had been directed to do, over the Prairie, where there was no trace of a path, and where the bay was concealed from sight by a narrow border of shrubbery along the shore, we struck off to the right, and had to search for some time before we could find a passage through the thick bushes. Having passed these, we found ourselves on the bay shore, with a broad expanse of water before us, and perceived upon the surface, at the distance of half a mile, the stake outside of which we were to pass. Cautiously, and not without some apprehensions, therefore, we made the best of our way towards it, several times narrowly escaping places where the mud was soft enough to mire or "stall" our horses, as it is called, through water, most of the way up to their bellies.

We were now avoiding the bayou, by riding in the direction of a salient angle into the lake : a pretty way, one would think, to keep out of the water. This was, however, the best route ; for the bayou, as it would seem, deepens its mouth, and forms something like a shoal or bar at a distance in advance, which the people have had the sagacity to find, and the boldness to follow, though concealed by the turbid water. The mud holes were all that gave us much solicitude ; for the horses being active, and all accustomed to the water, we knew they would swim well : but if their feet became entangled in the bottom, there would be danger of their plunging, and throwing us over their heads.

After passing the stake, we directed our course to the left, and having reached the land, proceeded along the Prairie to Mr. Heyne's house, the only habitation within many miles. The situation of his land is peculiar, being so entirely isolated, that the cattle require no fences to keep them from straying. The house stands near Old River, about half a mile above the junction with the Trinity, and there a quarter of a mile wide, with an extensive view over a fine Prairie, which affords a free range and rich pasturage to three or four hundred head of cattle. The proprietor had gone to Anahuac with his son, in his boat, a distance by water of about three or four miles. The land route is circuitous, and much farther. We were received by his wife and daughter, and introduced into their house. Not far off we observed the Dairy, which was a very simple establishment, consisting merely of wooden troughs, elevated a few feet from the ground, with no other covering from the weather and the sky but a few boards.

It was about noon when we arrived at this place; and after a short stop we proceeded on our way. But on reaching Trinity river, a little below the mouth of Old River, we found the water rather low; and the banks being abrupt, as is usual with the streams which run through the Prairies, our horses refused to plunge.   We got a boat and tried to lead them in : but were foiled in every attempt.   We now found ourselves at a stand, through the perverseness of our animals.   We presumed that a leap into deep water, from an elevation of only three or four feet, would be but a small inconvenience to a mustang under ordinary circumstances, especially to one which could leap seven or eight feet into a canoe or a ferry boat : but all our exertions were entirely fruitless, and we at length reluctantly returned to spend the night at the habitation we had left.

On our return to Heyne's we found two of the agents of the Galveston Bay and Texas Land Company, residing at Anahuac, who had been up Trinity river in a boat, in pursuit of two of the settlers they had brought from the United States, who had deserted them, alleging that they did not comply with their contract : a charge too true, though not on account of any fault of the agents. They had not been successful in their pursuit, and had stopped here a little while on their return.   We obtained some information from them, concerning the place to which we were bound ; and after they had left us, Mr. Heyne returned in his boat.

He is a native of the United States, but was for several years a soldier in the Mexican army, and abounds in anecdotes of an entertaining character, having seen much of this part of the world.   He

has resided here five or six years, and possesses a
tract of about a square league, which, like most of
the proprietors I have seen, who prefer their own, he
thinks a little the best tract in Texas. Other estates
are good, some very good indeed: but on the whole
this is rather preferable to any of them. We had
a good deal of conversation; and in the morning
were accompanied by our host to the river, to help
us across with our horses. Having more experience
than ourselves, he succeeded in getting one of our
animals, though much against his will, to leap from
the bank, and swim after the boat, while we held
the bridle. The others, mustang-like, soon determined to make the best of a bad bargain, and taking to
the water swam after us to the other side, where
they were caught and remounted. We then took
leave, and entered a bottom, or range of woodland,
on our way to Anahuac.

The appearance of the trees, and their fine shade
struck us with pleasure, the thermometer being
that day at 70° in the morning, and 80° at noon.
The growth was large, and consisted principally of
pine and cypress, with some cedar, ash, peccan, oak,
and walnut, and a little locust. A ride of twelve
miles brought us to Turtle Bayou, or river, a small
stream, which we crossed, and then entered an
extensive Prairie.

The "bottoms" of the rivers are of various
breadths on different streams, and at different places,

from a few rods, to ten or even twenty miles, and often form an important feature in the landscape, while they comprise in a great measure the country's resources in timber : the trees near the rivers in this region, being generally of the various kinds above enumerated, and placed near streams on which they may be floated.

On coming out of a low canebrake, we had another start, such as I had had several times before in this country. As we were riding carelessly along, a deer which had lain down in the canes, directly in our track, suffered us to approach till our mustangs almost trod upon him before he moved. The wind being against us, he had not scented us ; and therefore was roused only by their steps when very near. He then started from the ground with a sudden bound, while our horses sprung almost as far in the opposite direction, and we were all thrown into momentary confusion. The timid and active animal, according to the universal practice of his species, as far as I have had opportunity to observe, stopped a moment, turned back his head, and calmly surveyed us. His graceful form, smooth skin, and slender legs, we had hardly an instant to contemplate, when raising his head and tail with a snapping noise, he sprung away like the wind, and was out of sight almost as suddenly as he had made his appearance. Such occurrences, though frequent, seemed always to take us by surprise.

Every where in the Prairie were to be seen traces of the fire by which it had been overrun and devastated only a few weeks before. The young grass had begun to spring, but it was not yet high enough entirely to conceal the blackened surface and thin layers of ashes which contributed to its luxuriance. In one place however we came to a considerable tract of ground where the fire had not been, as it was overgrown with a thick cane brake about five feet high. So far apparently from all habitations, and in the midst of a region which had been but lately swept by the flames, we never thought that any evil could arise from a little amusement of the kind; and feeling curious to see the burning of a Prairie, we determined to set a small portion of it on fire. Dismounting therefore, by snapping our guns we soon obtained a flame, which we touched to a few of the tall canes, at this season as dry as fish-poles, and were surprised at the rapidity with which it spread. It rose fast in the air to their tops, communicating with others around, and soon began to roar and extend with greater and greater rapidity.

In an instant a loud report was heard, like the discharge of a horse pistol, in the midst of the fire, and then another, another and another, until they succeeded each other incessantly, as the flames spread and rose in a sheet above the highest canes in the brake. This was caused by the rarefaction of the air imprisoned in the joints of the reeds, the heat giving it an expansive force sufficient to make an explosion. The first moment had convinced us that we had set an element at work which we could by no means restrain; and the increased rushing of the wind around us, with the snapping of the canes, and the roar of the flames, as they swept away before us towards the heart of the boundless brake, impressed us with serious feelings, very different from those we had inconsiderately consulted in applying fire to such a mass of fuel.

As we stood gazing at the effects of our sport, the conflagration fast retired from us, levelling a broad track before us, where nothing was to be seen but a smooth, blackened and smoking surface, between two walls of standing canes. We now for the first time began to ask, whether there might not be some habitation in its path, or at least some person or domestic animal, exposed to be surrounded and burnt to death in an instant; but as it was evidently out of our power to do any thing to stop the devastation which we had commenced, we remounted and pursued our way. We often turned back to see the progress of the fire, which at length was to be traced only by a distant column of smoke rising from the vast level around us; and we could but flatter ourselves that no serious consequences would result from it.

CHAPTER X.

Anahuac.—Situation.—Galveston Bay.—Neighboring settlements.—
Soil, products, wild animals, fowl and fish.—" Shining the eyes."
Hunting by torchlight.—Pursuit of a murderer.—Character of the
Mexican troops at this post.

It was Saturday, the 26th of March, when we
reached Anahuac. It is a spot which had been
recently occupied as a military post, at General Teran's order, by his second in command in the eastern
military department of the Republic, Colonel Bradburn, with about an hundred soldiers. It had before
been known as Perry's Point, and now received the
name given to the city of Mexico by the original
inhabitants of the country. The situation is pleasant, at the north eastern corner of Galveston Bay,
on the verge of the Prairie, where the bank descends
abruptly from the water, about thirty feet : and looks
upon the bay, which spreads out about twenty
miles across, and sixty miles south, where it com-
municates with the Gulf of Mexico on both sides of
Galveston Island. The seven mouths of Trinity or
Trinidad river open into the bay near this corner,
and would offer important advantages of navigation
but for the bars, on which the water is sometimes

too shallow even for row boats. The tides are very small, but are sometimes considerably increased by strong southerly gales, which also occasionally render the water too brackish for use. We found fifteen or twenty log houses and huts, and seven poor shops, with the building erected as barracks for the garrison. This was about one hundred and fifty feet long and twenty wide, with the Colonel's quarters at one end, and the guard house at the other.

The country in the rear, perfectly level, generally green and beautifully variegated with groves and islands of trees, has a poor soil, of that sort which is called hog-bed Prairie; but yet it is capable of producing considerable crops even with the least possible labor. Indian corn, if merely dropped into holes, made with a stick, will grow and yield pretty well even without hoeing. There are very few inhabitants in this vicinity, and these are principally settlers from the United States, who have large scattering estates, and confine their attention almost exclusively to raising cattle. There is one estate a little off the road by which we came, which we had passed without observing, and another some miles south eastward from Anahuac. The former belongs to Mr. Taylor White, who has three thousand head of cattle. These are fed upon the Prairies which extend for many miles eastward from his residence, on the way to Nacogdoches. For the live stock a market is found at New-Orleans; and drovers annually visit this part of the country to purchase cattle, which they take back in great numbers.

Sugar and cotton flourish on proper soil. Judge Williams, who has an estate on Trinity river, some miles up, the previous year raised cane enough to make forty hogsheads of sugar of fine quality. The ribband cane requires to be planted every three years. The creole cane will continue to grow from the roots for ten or fifteen, and is but little' inferior to it.

Wild fowl are abundant hereabouts at this season: particularly geese and brandt, which form vast flocks, whose noise may be heard several miles. There are also ducks, pelicans, snipes, cranes, eagles, hawks, buzzards, owls, wild turkies, and many smaller birds. Deer are numerous in the Prairies, and sometimes appear in large herds: "but something else than a city huntsman," as one of the agents remarked, "is necessary to kill them." One is sometimes obliged to approach them through the grass for a mile, stooping almost to the ground and proceeding with the utmost caution. The turkies chiefly resort to the woods, where also are found wolves, bears, panthers, wild cats, wild hogs, foxes, rackoons, and squirrels. Wild cats and panthers are rather scarce, and never attack men unless very hungry or hard pressed at bay. The wild hog is very fierce, and, it is said, will generally attack a man even unprovoked.

The fish are various and numerous. Among them are several kinds which we never see at the north. The red fish is excellent, and quite large: weighing from ten to fifty pounds. Besides these are the buffalo fish, cat fish, drum fish, perch, oysters, crabs, &c. Alligators are unfortunately numerous in the bay and neighboring streams, and are found of various sizes. There is also the alligator garr: a singular animal: in form half fish and half alligator.

Large game is sometimes hunted in the night, in a manner common in the south western states, by what is called "shining," or "shining the eyes." The huntsman carries a lighted torch on his head, or sometimes a quantity of burning combustibles in a frying pan behind him, resting the handle on his shoulder, and has his rifle ready in his hand. Animals are attracted by a bright fire in the dark, and their eyes reflect the light so strongly, that they are perceptible, like sparks or coals, from a considerable distance. The position of the light prevents the huntsman from being distinctly seen, though at the same time it does not dazzle his own sight; and while the deer, bear, or other game stands gazing with wonder, he has an opportunity to take deliberate aim. This practice however is not unattended with danger: as it is impossible under such circumstances, to discriminate with certainty between the eyes of wild beasts and those of domestic animals; and in some parts of our own country, as in Kentucky for instance, wherever there are many settlements, hunting in this manner is forbidden by law.

A ludicrous hunting party on this plan was called out on the Prairie one night about the time of my visit at Anahuac. Some of the sportsmen in the huts and barracks were waked by the cries of the dogs, which had evidently brought some animal to a stand near by. They yelled so merrily, that numbers were soon out with their rifles and fowling pieces, half dressed, and scampering off to the spot. There they found the dogs barking up a tree, where the shade was deep, and where they looked long before they could perceive any thing. At length, by lighting a fire they discovered a pair of eyes shining far above them; and their pieces were immediately raised, supposing they had treed a rackoon. Colonel Bradburn, however, who was among the foremost of the hunters, suddenly ordered all to lower their guns; and sending up one of his Mexican soldiers, recovered a favorite kitten, which had strayed from his quarters, and having been pursued by the dogs, had caused this muster, and incurred so narrow a risk of its own life.

About the same time occurred a more serious hunt on the Prairie, whose causes and results were both far more important and painful. One of the emigrants entered his hut one day, and in a fit of violent passion wounded his wife in a shocking manner with an axe, so that she died a few days after. He immediately fled on foot across the Prairie: but the facts being known, a pursuit was soon commenced. A Virginian, a practised hunter, who was at Anahuac at the time, was among the first to learn the tidings; and seizing his rifle and springing upon his horse, called his hounds and dashed after him at full speed. The indignation and horror felt by all at the perpetration of such a crime, produced a general excitement: but there was something grotesque in the appearance made by this man, which might almost have provoked a smile: his long hair streaming in the wind from under his hat, and his cries and shouts to his dogs, which joined their voices to his own. The wretched fugitive, finding his pursuers fast gaining on him, though he had had the start by about a mile and a half, began to seek concealment, and was suddenly lost to their sight. The dogs however soon nosed out his hiding place; and when he was drawn out of the bushes, some of the hottest of his capturers were ready to kill him on the spot. He was however taken back to the town, and confined in the prison, (or calaboza, as a dungeon is called in Spanish,) to await his trial.

This man was subsequently offered a reprieve on condition that he should enlist in the Mexican army, to which he consented; and a few months afterwards lost his life.

The common soldiers at this post were men of a

most depraved character, while they were believed to
be as cowardly as they were wicked and ignorant.
The Mexican laws provide for the enlistment of
convicted criminals, of some of the worst kinds, into
the army; and the consequence is, that not a few of
the soldiers, especially those stationed at remote posts
like this, are men who would have suffered the
severest punishments in our own country. Many
of these are murderers, known, and publicly condemned as such. One of them, notorious for having
murdered not less than eleven persons, I often saw.
He was advanced in age, and died about this time,
by falling into shallow water where he was filling a
pail, being drowned before he was observed.

Some anxiety was expressed, by persons who
had observed smoke rising from a distant part of the
Prairie, lest a fire, kindled there as was to be supposed by accident, might cause some injury before it
should be extinguished. We were still not without
apprehensions ourselves: for we knew too well the
origin of the conflagration, but being unwilling to
incur blame when no good could result from it, 'we
were not forward to recount our experiment with the
cane brake. The smoke continued to rise for two
or three days, appearing every few hours in a different direction, as the wind drove the fire hither and
thither as often as it changed.

CHAPTER XI.

WHEN I left New-York, the greatest enthusiasm had existed among numbers of persons whom I saw, on the colonization of Texas. A number of young men had been engaged, by the Galveston Bay and Texas Land Company, to visit this part of the country as agents, under prospects which many more considered very flattering, and would probably have been glad to accept. They had anchored in the bay on the 18th of February, in the schooner Angelica, Capt. Fullerton, which sailed on the 29th of December, with thirty-four emigrants, chiefly Germans recently from Europe, men, women and children. Here they were, uncertain what to do, and with every prospect of being compelled to return, without accomplishing their object, viz: the settlement of the emigrants upon land claimed by their employers. General Teran, the military commander in chief of the eastern department of the Mexican Republic, in the name of the United Mex-

8*

ican States, refused to allow their claims or to
recognize the company, while he declared that the
law of Congress of the 6th of April annulled all
grants to empresarios which had not been fulfilled,
and of course destroyed all those which the company
professed to have consolidated. The authorities of
the state of Coahuila and Texas, had expressed
themselves favorably disposed : but there was no
prospect that this would prove of any advantage
under the existing circumstances. Indeed the state
surveyor and commissioner, who occasionally visited
Anahuac, continued to grant and set off land on the
tracts claimed by the company during their stay, on
the easy terms provided for by law.

The agents had encountered considerable difficulties as well as risks, in getting up to this place, with
their emigrants, luggage and cargo ; and had been
merely allowed to erect huts and to pitch tents for
their temporary accommodation ; but had not been
able to obtain any land, except about an acre and a
half on the shore, for a sort of garden, and a tract on
a farm about six miles up the Trinity river, which
they hired of inhabitants of the country. Colonel
Bradburn, General Teran's second in command,
who was stationed at Anahuac, being a North Amer
ican by birth, treated them with kindness, but was
peremptory in dealing with them according to superior orders. Their situation was consequently very
unpleasant. Being young men, inexperienced in

business of this kind, but spirited, enterprizing and disposed, as I thought, to spare no pains in the honorable execution of their duties, they had embarked in the project with great confidence in the directors of the company, and in full expectation of finding the country open to their entrance and occupation. The emigrants had formed contracts with the company, by which they were to be furnished with a "labor," or one hundred and seventy-seven acres and a fraction of land each, as their own, and supplied with tools and one year's subsistence, on condition of settling under them, and working for the company two days in a week the first year.

The agents had found, on their arrival, that the company were almost entirely ignorant of the country, and totally uninformed concerning existing settlements and claimants.* They had discovered

* The instructions given to the agents were of such a nature, that their perusal would probably have surprised purchasers.

First, they denominate themselves "the Attornies and Trustees of Lorenzo de Zavala, Joseph Vehlein and David G. Burnet, Empresarios of certain grants of land made by the Federal Governments of Mexico and the state of Coahuila and Texas." These "grants," as has been already remarked, were very different things from what usually bear this name.

The signers, that is, two of the Trustees, then remark that they rely on their efforts to carry their views and plans into effect. Their plans appear from the instructions to have been—to obtain information concerning the country, bays, rivers, &c., with the names of settlers, their claims, their disposition to take titles from the company, &c., to draw two base lines north and south, survey and lay off labors and sitios on both sides of them, making that they had no power to perform the stipulations of the company towards the emigrants, or to provide for the future comfort or subsistence of those poor and helpless strangers.   They still however appeared to be exerting themselves to do the best they could, both to quell and to prevent discontent, conducting with moderation and courtesy towards the authorities of the country, and taking every judicious measure as agents, both towards their employers and towards the colonists.   They were very anxious

reservations for villages, to place the first settlers on them, and make them till the reservations for the company. They required information on so many points, as to prove that they had no particular knowledge of the coast, settlements or inhabitants, and even no certainty whether the agents and colonists could land on any part of Galveston Bay or the rivers flowing into it. They instruct the agents on landing, to "endeavor to find, from any person on the premises, if there is any one or more persons claiming title to the land; if so, under whom." "You will for the present respect all claims," &c.—"If the land adjoining the water in every direction is claimed by any person, endeavor to make an arrangement so as to effect a landing with all despatch, and to secure a place for all future emigrants going to that country. Ascertain how far the claimants' rights extend, and if there is any land on the water not claimed on which it is advisable to locate. Make your first lodgment on it, whether it be on the bay side, Trinity river, or east side of San Jacinto river. Be careful in all cases to give no assurances, and express no opinion as to the validity of any claim to land which may be set up by actual settlers or others, *except* where you find any person claiming under John Lucius Woodbury; then you must give them notice to quit the premises."

It is not calculated to make a man feel any particular pride in his own sagacity, who finds persons talking confidentially in terms like these, of property they have professed to sell to him.

and somewhat dissatisfied at not receiving letters
from the Company, and thought their silence very
extraordinary, as they must have known that further
instructions would be necessary, and had promised
them. This silence afterwards proved very disheartening, as several vessels arrived from New-York,
as well as New Orleans. Some suspicions began
to be afloat, to fear that this party had been sent
out merely for effect, to promote the sale of stock
and scrip, without any intention of following up
such a regular system of colonization, which they
had been led to expect: and thus the agents had
to meet a variety of trials.

An incident had occurred a little calculated to
shake the faith of the agents and emigrants when
it was known. When on the eve of sailing from
New-York, it was accidentally discovered, that the
contracts of the Company with the emigrants were
not signed. They were immediately taken to one
of the Trustees, and afterwards sent down, and
distributed to them again, as was supposed, complete.
The attention of the agents was not again directed
to this subject, until one of the emigrants resigned
his contract at New Orleans, and left the vessel. It
was then found that they were all signed by only
one of the Trustees, although it was expressly stated
in the body of these instruments, that two signatures
should be necessary to render them binding. This
circumstance excited only a little surprise at the

time, and might have been owing to accident: but
with other things, afterwards helped to raise ques-
tions and speculations.

As I received friendly treatment from these gentlemen, and had opportunities to witness the trying
condition in which the poor emigrants were placed,
as well as to see their own exertions in the discharge
of their duty amidst the discouragements around
them, I could not but feel a lively interest in them,
and regret that they should have shared with me in
the evil consequences of confiding too far in men's
characters and declarations. Doubly did the situation of some of the Germans seem to appeal to our
sympathy. Ignorant of every thing, especially of
the country, they had gone blindly into a wild expedition, committed themselves to the hands of a
company, bound themselves by their signatures,
and received in return papers which they could not
read, under the full belief that they thus acquired
good titles to little estates, though they in fact obtained
what was of no value whatever. Here they were,
hutted under leaky boards, some with their wives
and little children, in a strange land, without any
means of providing for the future, and believing
that they had been made dupes by persons whom
they had never injured or provoked, and whom they
had scarcely seen. It seems to me, that if a speculator,
in the eager pursuit of gold, could have visited these
poor creatures, and heard their complaints, seen their

depression, disappointment and misery, and at the same time realized their melancholy prospect, perhaps not yet certainly anticipated by them, of sinking under the disease which periodically infests this part of the country, he would have been careful how he ever involved the poor and confiding, the stranger and the foreigner, by any schemes for self-aggrandizement.

I did not make up my mind that the Company had acted on any concerted plan to injure the agents or the emigrants. That would have required evidence which I could not obtain in those circumstances. But I heard and saw enough to become persuaded, that the results of their operations had been disastrous and were likely to be more so: while on the one hand they appeared to have acted with little knowledge of what they had been supposed to be well informed of, and on the other, by their silence, seemed unaccountably indifferent to the expedition and all connected with it.

What was calculated to add, if any thing could well add, to the mortification of such circumstances, to those who were Protestants, was the knowledge which they did not obtain until their arrival, that they could not settle in the country, without avowing themselves Roman Catholics. It has been said that the Mexican government will protect our citizens in life and property so long as they conform to the laws, as if this would avoid the necessity of changing

their religious profession. But this has nothing to
do with the case. The treaty, in the article sometimes quoted, alludes only to our citizens residing in
Mexico, not to colonists, who must become Mexican
citizens; and whose submission to the laws relating
to colonization implies the profession of the Roman
Catholic religion. Whatever laxity may occur in
executing the laws at any period, they may be at any
time put in force; and what I afterwards saw at
San Felipe proves how the subject is viewed by persons on the ground. If known as Protestants, they
might at any time be deprived of their estates by the
execution of laws still unrepealed.

CHAPTER XII.

On the 28th of March, the third day after my arrival at Anahuac, I accepted, with one of my companions, an invitation to accompany two of the agents of the Land Company, to take a sail to Galveston or St. Luis Island, off the mouth of the bay. We laid in provisions of salt pork, bread, and coffee, for a few days, but were disappointed in having no wind. We, however, took advantage of what is sometimes called the " ash breeze :" that is, our oars, and proceeded down the bay at a pretty good rate.

The agents had encountered much difficulty, and some hazard, in getting their vessel over the bar on their arrival; but having heard that a deep channel existed, by which even ships of war had heretofore entered, had determined to seize an early opportunity to sound out the ground, for the information of their company, and the convenience of future vessels. I was anxious to receive news from the United States;

and the agents expressed great concern at the want
of instructions from their employers, as their circumstances had been rendered doubly embarrassing by
the arrival of the agents and emigrants sent out by
the Union Company, for which they had been totally
unprepared. This Company, as was represented,
consisted of persons who held shares of stock purchased from the Galveston Bay and Texas Land
Company, and had sent them out to commence a
settlement on some of the grants. At the same
time, they communicated nothing which might
enable the other agents to proceed in relation to
them with confidence ; and gave them to understand
that they preferred to act independently of them.
The two parties treated each other with proper
respect and cordiality as individuals ; and had united
in sending a mutual agent to Matamoras in the
Angelica, to represent their interests to General
Teran: but the first agents did not officially recognize
the existence of any such Company as their compet-
itors claimed to represent.

We spent most of the day in rowing down the
bay ; when, about half an hour before sunset, we
discovered the sloop Chauncey, of whose arrival we
had not heard, coming up from sea. Presuming
that we had letters on board, we steered for her
immediately, and rowed hard that we might reach
her before dark. We continued to approach her
pretty rapidly, until after about an hour, on turning

to look for her, we found she had become enveloped
in a mist, and we could not perceive any trace of
her. After a little hesitation, we determined to make
the best of our way for the land; and, raising our
sail, put our boat off before the wind, judging that
although we were some miles from the eastern
shore, we must reach it pretty early in the night.
We were now in a more serious situation than we
had anticipated, on engaging in this excursion of
pleasure; for to such inexperienced watermen as
several of us were, having hardly ever attempted to
feather an oar before this morning, it appeared rather
a gloomy task to sit exposed in a light little boat,
upon a broad sheet of water, whose shores we could
not see, and of which we were almost entirely ignorant.

After proceeding in this manner for two or three
hours, our anxiety began to increase: for we found
we had miscalculated our distance, and apprehended
that we might be proceeding in a direction where we
should experience some difficulty. And the time
seemed very long before we saw any land: for it
was not until twelve o'clock, that we found ourselves
upon a beach formed of loose shells, and bordered by
a low grove of trees. We landed immediately; and
drawing the boat upon the beach, began to explore
the unknown country. The first view of the place
impressed us with the belief that we were on the
borders of a garden, as the foliage seemed like that

of fruit trees ; and we hoped to find some hospitable
mansion, where we might pass the rest of the night.
We found, however, that the trees were a growth of
shrub oaks, intermingled with the nopal, or rock
pear, which I had seen in the Northern States
growing only to the height of six or eight inches,
and now looked on with surprise, ten or fifteen feet
in height, in this more genial region. This vegetable,
which is fed on by the insect that yields the cochineal
dye, has been adopted by the Mexicans as their
national plant, and introduced into their coat of
arms with the eagle.   There are two kinds, bearing
fruit shaped like a pear, of different colors.   Further
examination satisfied us that the shore was uncul-
tivated ; and as the air was mild, we stretched
ourselves upon the dry beach, and being fatigued,
soon fell into a refreshing sleep.   These shores are
generally infested by musquitoes, even at this season
of the year : but fortunately the wind was fresh
enough through the night to prevent them from
annoying us.

In the morning we awoke to enjoy the sight of
sunrise, though in a somewhat cloudy sky, over a
level and extensive shore, with the spacious bay of
Galveston in view, but not, as we had supposed,
immediately before us. We were on the southern
bank of a narrow creek, which at the distance of a
mile west of us joined the bay ; and on referring to
our map, we found that its name was Oyster bayou,

and that it was at no great distance from the Gulf
of Mexico. We had gone much further to the
southward than we had supposed, during the night's
sail, and our boat had been driven by the wind,
without our suspecting it, a considerable distance
inland. The thick shrubbery presented less of its
artificial appearance by daylight: but there were
several beautiful groves seen at no great distance on
the green, level Prairie behind us, which had much
the appearance of art well applied. One of these
particularly attracted my attention. It consisted of
forty or fifty fine forest trees, rising with smooth and
straight stems from the uniform level, and forming a
thick mass of shade, with little appearance of underbrush to obstruct a path beneath. There was so
much in the aspect of this spot to associate it with
the idea of man, that I set off with my fowling
piece in my hand, to visit the habitation which I
fully expected to find on the opposite side. Passing
rapidly over the smooth and verdant level, and
through the little wood, I could scarcely credit my
sight, when I found the opposite side lonely and
destitute of all signs of habitation.

We found the snipe and plover very numerous,
and soon shot about twenty brace, which were roast-
ed for breakfast by a fire kindled on the beach; and,
having made some coffee, we enjoyed a fine meal.
We also discovered that the bayou had not received
its name at random: for as the tide fell we saw

9*

great quantities of oysters of the ordinary size, which proved to be well flavored. We collected as many as we could well carry in our boats in a few minutes, but not without wading some distance into the water, as there we found the finest, although there were many left dry upon the beach. We rowed some distance; and then hoisting our sail, proceeded with a north westerly wind, through the mouth of the bay across the strait which intervenes between it and Galveston Island, where we arrived at noon. There, drawing up our boat, we employed a few minutes in shooting at the birds around us; when, having got enough for a dinner, we cooked and ate them with a good appetite.

The island is thirty-six miles in length, from one to three wide, and presents nothing like a landmark except a hut in one spot, and three small trees, which grow in a cluster near the western end, and offer a beacon to mariners. We found the island a mere sand bank of vast extent, with an unvarying surface, thinly covered with grass and weeds, having been recently burnt over, under Colonel Bradburn's directions. It is said to abound with rattle and moccasin snakes. The ground was still partly blackened, and we killed a rattlesnake with seven rattles, and five feet long. We took a long walk, having plenty of time, and probably went not less than ten or twelve miles. During the excursion we started a solitary deer, which fled off with great

speed; and afterwards picked up a large collection
of beautiful shells which are scattered in abundance
along the beach. Deer and wolves are said to
abound here.

Here the famous pirate Lafitte so long made his
rendezvous; and somewhere in the vicinity of the
three trees, it is reported, he concealed his ill-gotten
money in the earth. One of his men, whom I
saw at Anahuac, told me that he sometimes brought
vessels drawing sixteen feet of water into the bay.
This may have been possible, for the loose sands
between the island and the main land may be easily
shifted by the currents; and the high tides driven in
by southerly winds sometimes raise the water several
feet.

The hut mentioned above, had been erected by
soldiers from Anahuac, at Colonel Bradburn's order,
for the accommodation of a guard usually kept
there, with a flag flying. We visited it, and found
several of those dark complexioned, inefficient looking men employed in jerking beef, which they had
purchased of some of the nearest settlers. They
cut the meat into long strings, which they dry
thoroughly in the sun, and then lay aside for use.
We were kindly received by the soldiers. While
cooking our supper, we received an invitation from
the master of the Chauncey, which was not far off, to
spend the night on board, which we accepted.

On the following morning we took our boat,

and sounded out the western channel of the eastern entrance into Galveston bay. From its entrance Point Bolivar bears N. N. W. It is three quarters of a mile wide, approaches the shore of the island within two hundred yards, and has from three to five fathoms of water all the way in. On the western breaker the soundings are six feet. On getting inside of the island, there is found a beautiful and convenient harbor, sheltered from all winds, being protected by Point Bolivar on the east, and Pelican Island on the north, with enough water for a vessel drawing sixteen feet. From this place up to Redfish Bar, we proceeded in the lighter. It is twenty-five miles from Anahuac. We had from seven to nine feet water all the way. On that bar, at low tides there is but three or four feet, and at the highest tides not more than five feet eight inches.

The tides in this bay are so small as sometimes to appear to be entirely dependant on the winds. The north winds, or "northers," which prevail with greater force in the fall and winter, often render the upper parts very shallow.

We stopped at Col. Edwards's fine estate, opposite Redfish Bar, in the morning; and after spending some time in fishing and catching crabs, saw a schooner, just arrived from New Orleans, going to Harrisburgh, and boarded her with our boat. In her we found a wine merchant from New-York, who wished to visit Anahuac, and accepted of an invitation to accompany us. We soon after set sail with him, but were overtaken by night in the midst of the bay. We steered as well as we could towards our port, until I was overcome with drowsiness, and although the wind was violent, and the spray flying over us, I fell asleep. On waking I found it was total darkness, the boat was rocking and pitching worse than before, and my companions were in consternation, not knowing what to expect. We were all wet to the skin ; but much relieved, when, about midnight we felt the boat ground in the mud. Jumping out we soon found the shore, and drawing up the boat and kindling a roaring fire we stretched ourselves under the high bank and were soon asleep. Morning found us in a state of great uncertainty. On the question whether we should go north or south to find Anahuac, we were of directly opposite opinions ; so that we could agree on nothing but to go inland and make observations. We were soon divided into parties, and took different routes. I had not gone far with my companions, when we met two men and a woman travelling to the mouth of the Brazos, who set us right. In a short time we found our way in our boat to Anahuac, about two or three miles distant.

CHAPTER XIII.

Anahuac.—State Cavalry.—Tuscasito.—A Texas election.—Mr. Taylor White's estate.—The farm hired by the Union Company.—Driving cattle.—Experiment in driving a herd of Mr. White's.—Another accomplishment of my mustang.—An alligator.

CAPTAIN Zebulon Pike, who visited Texas in 1807, had little opportunity to make observations, as he was carried across it as a prisoner, having been captured by the Spaniards on the Rio Bravo for violating their territory, which he did in consequence of mistaking that stream for the Red river, with a small party of American soldiers under his command. Among his remarks is one of this nature: that the Mexicans are capable of making excellent troops. The truth of this would have been denied by me if I had seen only the soldiers of Colonel Bradburn: but a few dragoons who were sent to Anahuac from Bexar by the authorities of the state, were much better looking men, and inclined me to raise my opinion somewhat of the talents of their countrymen. They were not men of bad character, like the soldiers of the general government, but of better appearance and some of them pretty well educated. One in particular had spent several years in Kentucky, and possessed an amiable disposition as well as an intelligent mind, calculated to procure esteem. These dragoons were perhaps the best horsemen I ever saw, and appeared remarkably well in the saddle. No matter how much their horses might prance and curvet, leap or run, their riders kept their saddles with firmness and grace, and it seemed impossible to displace them. They had evidently been long habituated to riding, and were always ready to lend their aid in pursuing any run-away horse that had taken to the Prairie, whenever the owner found difficulty in recovering him. One or two of them would spur off with lazo in hand, race with the fugitive, and on approaching him throw the noose over his head and rein up to stand the shock if necessary, and generally returned with their captive in a state of abject submission.

To hear the names by which certain places are sometimes designated in this vicinity, or to see them written on a map, one might be led into great errors concerning the state of the country. Tuscasito, instead of being a town or even a village, is a mere stopping place on the way to San Antonio, with a single house and a blacksmith's shop. It is situated on a sand Prairie, where are hardly any signs of vegetation, yet where Indian corn will grow, and look well if barely put into the ground, though it will not yield a large harvest. I have heard it said that forty bushels to an acre is a very great crop on that tract.   The view from that spot is fine, looking out upon the bay.   Mr. George Orr, who has lived there several years, has a family of fine children ; but there is no other inhabitant in the vicinity.   The spot is important to travellers ; and there is a yard for horses, which is a very unusual thing.

An election was held there about the time of our visit to Anahuac, at which settlers from a great extent of the surrounding country assembled, all, or nearly all North Americans.   It was held on the Sabbath, according to the common custom in Mexico ; the polls were opened in Spanish and English, and tellers having been appointed, voting went on. One old man of ninety had come on horseback about sixty miles.   This "republican" meeting was held in a small log building just erected for a court house ; in the rear of which a cart was backed up on the Prairie, with a barrel of whiskey in it, furnished with a spigot, and free to all.

An alcalde who was elected in another place, I was informed, was one of my own countrymen, and had fled from the United States for murder.

Mr. Taylor White, one of the wealthiest inhabitants in this part of Texas, has a fine estate on the Prairie about five miles from Anahuac.   I visited it several times, and once in company with a physician, newly arrived from the United States, who had been sent for to Anahuac to pay a professional visit to one of his family.   Some idea may be formed of the scarcity of medical science in the country, and the abundance of beef, when I mention that the fee paid for this single visit was a cow!

The agents of the Union company had hired a tract on the estate of Mr. White, for a farm, having, like the rival company, no other way to obtain even the use of land, though they professed to have many square leagues for sale. They employed some of their emigrants upon it, and things appeared flourishing there, as well as on other parts of the estate. We always brought home a few fresh vegetables, whenever we returned from Mr. White's, to add to our bill of fare in the city, as Anahuac was prospectively denominated. Mr. White's house stood a little in advance of a tract of woodland, which skirted a small stream or bayou. It was, of course, of logs, and faced the north, with an extensive Prairie scene before it, on which cattle, innumerable at such a distance, were straying among rich and abundant pasturage, sometimes singly and sometimes in considerable droves.

The outhouses belonging to this dwelling were such as to show that the owner had a number of laborers, and carried on a very extensive business as a cattle-raiser. His dairy, as usual, was comparatively small and ill furnished, being chiefly in the open air. The farmers of Texas commonly make some butter and cheese, at least enough for their own families, and have abundance of milk: but these

10

things engross but few of their thoughts. They
churn daily, and therefore are always supplied with
butter milk. They often regret it if they have no
"sour milk" to offer a visiter, and generally regale
him with it—which, whether denominated "bonny
clapper," or any thing else, I had ere this become
fond of, though in the endeavor to like it I had to
overcome a strong prejudice. I found sugar cane
and cotton both growing in small patches, with good
prospects of success, and understood that they had
flourished well before.

Finding Mr. White one day about going out
upon the Prairie to drive up his cattle, I mounted
my horse and accompanied him, to see something of
the way of managing these half wild animals. It
is customary to drive them up occasionally towards
the house, for different purposes; and thus the habit
of submission is not entirely forgotten. I found, as
on former occasions, that the cattle of Texas, notwithstanding their free manner of life, are in some
respects more manageable than our own. They
move more readily in herds, and yet more easily
suffer themselves to be singled out when the driver
wishes to separate particular animals. Their aspect
is however much wilder and more spirited than that
of our own, especially when they become excited
and rush together in a mass, as they sometimes do.
Occasionally one will begin to bellow; and this
seems to render the rest furious. They raise their

heads, hold their tails almost straight up in the air, and run violently towards the sound, often replying with similar bellowings, and thus collect by hundreds. In general, however, they are peaceable and quiet. Sometimes they are driven together by their owners, to have the calves separated ; and at other times they are collected for marking. Horsemen ride into the pen among them, and throw their lazos over the horns or necks of the young animals, which, in attempting to escape, dash themselves violently upon the ground, and become almost strangled; while advantage is taken of their temporary weakness and alarm, to apply the branding iron to their flanks and mark them for life. In this short process they appear to acquire that horror of the lazo which all the tame animals of Texas exhibit, and which is found in many of those wild oxen and horses which to a stranger might seem to have spent their lives in unrestrained freedom. It appears that this instrument of civilization gives a lesson which is seldom or never forgotten : for when the lazo falls over the head of an ox that has had experience with it before, he instantly stops, as I have remarked of the horses, and conducts with humility and submission until he feels it removed. This is the most convenient method possible of treating a refractory milch cow. I have seen them standing stock still at the pail with a lazo over their horns, though there was no actual force applied to detain them, when without it they would have set every thing at defiance.

The lazo was not resorted to on the occasion to which I referred, for there was no need of it. The cattle were to be only driven up near the house; and as there were several hundreds of them, I volunteered my assistance. Drawing my bridle towards them, I found my little horse no way loath to proceed to the business: on the contrary, he hastened after the herd, and soon made some of them quicken their pace. He even pressed upon them farther than I thought necessary, and at last began to bite such as he could reach. I now suspected that he had had much more experience than I had ever supposed, in the station of a mustang on a farm. And when an ox broke away from the drove, as one soon did, he was no more at a loss concerning his duty in such a case; and, taking a sudden turn, which almost twitched me out of my saddle, threw himself after the fugitive at full speed. The race was swift but short: for the ox finding itself out run, turned back to rejoin the herd. The pestilent little horse at the same time bolted once more, and (how I know not,) took me back with him: for I felt myself on the verge of an overthrow. It was not long before my watchful and busy little horse spied another deserter from the ranks; and off he sprang again sideways, without giving me the slightest notice, and scam-

pered over the Prairie, after one of the wild creatures
we were driving—then, in a moment, he was at
another full stop that almost threw me over his head,
and back again like the wind to his old place.

My strength and commands proved alike unavailing. Like a stubborn cook, who takes raw and
roast into her own hands, he was above my advice
and set my orders at naught, so that I was compelled
to swallow whatever he pleased to give me. He
had had experience in cattle-driving long before I
had ever seen Texas or a wild ox, and seemed to
have determined to show me how impudent and
provoking a mustang can be, under the mask of
faithful and untiring service in a job selected for him
by his master. I thought for sometime that I should
never get my bones back whole to Anahuac: for it
was not twice nor thrice that the cattle ran out of
the drove near us, and he invariably insisted on
giving chace to all estrays and bringing them back,
in his own peculiar style, or like a dog after sheep—
let me do or say what I would. At length, I
began to feel more at home in the business, and by
close attention kept myself better guarded against
his dodgings and doublings. It was not however
until the chace was over and I had dismounted, that
I felt perfectly safe.

Mr. White informed me that, although he had
been in the country but three or four years, he had
between three and four thousand head of cattle, of

10*

which but a small part were in sight. The great majority were straying through the bottoms and Prairies for many miles off towards the east, along the route to Nacogdoches. He sometimes sends out three or four men to collect, and mark them. This is called hunting cattle. What seems strange in such a state of things is, that it is a very rare thing to hear of cattle being stolen in Texas.

Returning from Mr. White's, with a friend, one day, we perceived a young alligator, about two feet and a half in length, on the dry land far from any water; and having lazoed him, by tying a noose in the horse's halters and throwing it over his head, we set out to lead him home with us. Soon however he appeared to lose his strength and then his life: suffering us to drag him without making any movement, sometimes on his back and some-times on his belly. As we supposed we must have nearly if not quite killed him by some accident, (it being far from our intention,) we threw him into a little puddle we passed near Anahuac, and left him. It happened however that on visiting the spot two or three hours afterwards, we found him in perfect health, and apparently good spirits, moving about as vigorous and active as ever. So having caught him again, we took him into the village. Colonel Bradburn had a bear tied to a tree, which to our surprise showed evident fear when this little crea-ture was brought near him; and when the alligator sprung towards him, as it did with a good deal of spite, he climbed up the tree as fast as possible and refused to come down again. After we had kept the alligator for a few days, it broke away from the halter one night, and effected its escape.

CHAPTER XIV.

Burning a Prairie.—Old pirates.—A dog and an alligator. Mexican colonization laws.—Powers of the Galveston Bay and Texas Land Company.—Disturbance among the soldiers.—Capture of a large alligator.

Two of my acquaintances here, were one day riding with Colonel Bradburn in the afternoon, when it was proposed to set the Prairie on fire. They separated from each other, and at distances of about half a mile, dismounted, struck fire, and kindled the dry grass which at that time covered the surface of the ground. It instantly began to flame ; and the fire, sweeping on before the wind, cut three paths through the grass, which was then about three feet high. The horsemen pursued their way between two of the fires ; and, by trotting briskly on, nearly kept pace with the flames. The darker the sky became, the brighter shone the light ; and the two lines of fire gradually approached each other, so that they at length came near, and blazed up bright on the right and left, and almost hedged up their way.

The scene was described as very splendid and striking. Even when viewed from a distance, the effect was brilliant ; and on the return of the

gentlemen to Anahuac they found the people attracted
by the light. Though about two miles and a half
off, the fire was distinctly visible, being then spread
over a great extent of the surface in a narrow band,
with the dark smoke above and the Prairie beneath,
so that it appeared something like the bright sky at
sunset, as we sometimes see it when a long cloud
stretches nearly to the horizon, and leaves a single
stripe of dazzling light.

The famous pirate Lafitte, as is well known, made
his rendezvous in Galveston Bay. Being familiar
with the channels round the island off its mouth, as
well as the anchorage just within, he had always a
safe and convenient retreat. Two of his men I
found at Anahuac. They were named Roach and
Franks. Roach told me, (what I understand passes
for the truth,) that he has often seen an eighteen
gun ship brought and anchored in the bay, though
now vessels of very moderate size are apt to strike
on the bar in coming in. Franks is above six feet
high, and remarkably expert in shooting a rifle. A
man who knew him well, I was informed, did not
hesitate to hold a board for him to shoot at from a
considerable distance.

I was on the shore one day when some bystanders
were sending a little dog into the water to attract an
alligator within shooting distance. Franks was
there with his rifle ; and made several good shots at
him, though no fatal ones. The little dog would

readily swim for chips which were thrown in : but as soon as he found the alligator approaching, would turn and retreat.

The thermometer ranged between 70° and 80° in the day time during my stay at Anahuac. The north winds are the coldest and most unhealthy here after the season of fevers begins, which is somewhat later than this time. Inhabitants represent them as being remarkably unfavorable to health. Children often begin to droop when they begin to blow ; and usually revive when a south breeze sets in ; and in cases of sickness adults are often sensibly affected by the changes. The temperature sometimes varies 40° in twenty-four hours. It is thought that the moss which we call Spanish moss, and use for stuffing mattresses, indicates an unhealthy region wherever it greatly abounds. The trees are much loaded with it about Anahuac ; and the place is no doubt very liable to fevers. Still, there can be no question that the climate hereabouts is far more healthy than the lower parts of the bordering United States.

I visited the garden spot which the agents were permitted by Colonel Bradburn to cultivate. It was situated on the point, a short distance from their quarters, and was an acre and a half in extent. It was overgrown with trees, which had to be cut down, before any thing could be planted : and then indeed the roots were so thick and numerous, that it was only here and there, where a little spot could be cleared by grubbing, that a few seeds could be planted. The soil was found to be as light and thin as on the Prairie; that is not more than six inches deep; but so favorable is the climate to vegetation, that the agents have been astonished at the rapid growth of vegetables planted. In truth, radishes may be had from the seed in a fortnight; water melons flourish to admiration, and ripen to within half an inch of the very rind, and are so wholesome that they are said not to injure those sick of fever. It is strange to have so light a soil prove so rich and productive, while it is so thin that beets, and other roots which penetrate beyond a few inches, will not grow. Of all this the agents had practical evidence during the season. The garden, when I saw it, was laid out with taste and planted partly with flowers, although interrupted by roots which the emigrants found too large for easy removal.

The more I reflected on the real state of things with respect to the grants, so called, the more I found reason to wonder at the course pursued in relation to them. No one who reads the official documents of the Mexican government, can pretend that the empresarios, or any of them, were authorised to proceed to the sale of land. They had obtained no title themselves, and they could not obtain any, except to the five-league tracts which they were to receive for every hundred settlers procured, and even

of this they could not hold above a certain quantity
over a fixed term of years, while none could they
hold until the settlers should have been long enough
upon the ground to comply with the requisition of
the laws. Of course the empresarios could not have
conferred a right which they did not themselves
possess : and whence then the power claimed by
the Company to sell land ? It may be argued, that
the Company have not expressly offered to sell
land; and one might question, after reading their
publications, whether they contain any claim clearly
and directly in opposition with the rights of the
empresarios. I have found some difficulty in as-
certaining exactly what claims the Company intend
to set up on this point. In their trust deed, as
published, the three empresarios have covenanted
and agreed to place their several grants of land and
contracts aforesaid, into one common stock, to be
held in trust, to and for the use of all the parties
interested therein, in the proportions in said instruments named, irrevocably in the hands and under
the control of the said Anthony Dey, William H.
Sumner, and George Curtis, and their successors,
for the purpose of surveying, locating, and setting
off the said territories and lands into settlements,
villages and towns ; and of giving, granting, selling,
colonizing, and otherwise disposing of, and managing
the same in such way and manner as they or the
majority of them shall deem best for the interest

of all the parties concerned, according to the power herein granted, and the authority in them vested by said agreements of even date herewith, and the articles of association hereto annexed."

They also, (as I understand the language of the deed,) for valuable considerations, gave, granted, bargained and sold, aliened, assigned, transferred and conveyed to the Company and their successors, "all the right, title, interest, property and estate" which the said parties of the first part have of, "in and to the grants and contracts before referred to," * * * * * "and to the lands in said grants described and contained, in our absolute and perfect possession and property being, and to all the privileges, emoluments and advantages arising or to arise from, by and under the same, or which are in any way incident thereto"—renouncing all interest, title, &c., except as members of the Company. I quote also the following expression :—"*to have and to hold* the above granted, bargained and described premises, and all our right, title and interest therein, and to all the lands and privileges in said grants contained and therefrom resulting"— * * * * "subject to the terms and conditions of said grants, and the provisions herein made and contained," to the articles of association, and future amendments and alterations.

The empresarios covenant that they "severally are the sole owners of the said grants and contracts

11

to us made ;" *   *   *   *   that they " are lawfully
seized of said grants and contracts," *   *   *   *
" have a good and perfect right to sell, and dispose
of, and alienate the same in manner aforesaid," &c.

Whether this instrument professes to confer a
right to sell the land or not, or what may have been
the intentions of the empresarios, I pretend not to
determine.   I can only say, that the Company must
have known what was the intention of the empresarios, and, what is of greater consequence, they must
have had the means of knowing what powers the
empresarios possessed over the land, if not what
right they had to transfer them.

That they did and do profess to sell land, however,
I presume will not be doubted.   The letter of which
the following is a copy, was addressed by one of the
Trustees of the Company to a gentleman I know.

My Dr. Sir,

"If you wish some of the Texas Lands,
" you can *now* have some at 10 cents—you can have
" one share in the *Company* of 10,000 acres, at
" $1000, at 6 months with interest; or if you desire
" it, you have a less quantity in scrip, at the same
" rate.   It appears to me whether purchased to sell
" again, or with a view to actual settlement, it cannot
" be otherwise than a most profitable investment.
" You can consider this offer as made to *you,* and if
" not disposed to avail yourself of it, you will of

" course be silent on the subject of it. Let me hear " from you this morning.

" Yours, &c."

(This is endorsed in another hand, January, 1831.)

It is not wonderful that the emigrants on arriving here, should have been discontented with the state of things in which they found themselves. Instead of 'entering upon the possession and occupancy of extensive estates which had been promised them, they could obtain no satisfaction to any of their enquiries or demands, beyond such indefinite and general statements as the agents, (in their state of uncertainty) could give them, about a final favorable result. Just at this time also a threatening difficulty took place among the Mexican troops, which caused them reasonable alarm. These miserable men, being chiefly condemned criminals, banished to a distant and solitary post for the punishment of various crimes, it might be presumed, would be ready for the perpetration of any thing for which sufficient temptation, and their own courage might prove sufficient.

During the absence of Colonel Bradburn, a worthless lieutenant celebrated his birth-day at Anahuac ; and becoming somewhat intoxicated, claimed the right of command instead of the commissary, who had to interfere to maintain his authority. The soldiers were in a state of great excitement, and had mustered in front of the barracks, cursing the " Americans," and threatening a revolt : for the lieutenant had taken care to work upon their prejudices. The commissary possessed great bold-ness ; and, knowing the cowardly character of those miserable troops, drew his sword and rushed in among them alone, with a few cuts and many demonstrations, ordering them into the barracks, which they at length obeyed, after a few of them had been wounded, but without daring to offer any resistance. The refractory lieutenant having been seized, pinioned, and thrown into the calaboza, the commissary informed the agents that they had better be prepared against any attack which the soldiers might be disposed to make on them in the night ; and the whole forces of the emigrants were immedi-ately called out, and stood in the rain for an hour or more, awaiting the movements of the profligate troops at the barracks. No further disturbance, however, occurred ; and though the colonists slept with their arms at their sides or under their pillows, they were not disturbed. Such an occurrence, how-ever, could not but add to the uncomfortable condition of the agents and emigrants, since a number of women and children were involved with them in all the difficulties by which they were surrounded. The lieutenant was afterwards indulged with a rustication at Galveston Island, under the charge of a file of soldiers.

Part of a farm had been hired by the agents of the Galveston Bay and Texas Land Company, of a colonist settled on the Trinity river. On approaching it, in company with a friend, on a visit, while walking along the bank of the river, we discovered, in a low, marshy spot sometimes overflown by the rising of the stream, the largest alligator I ever saw, lying motionless, like a great log. We ventured, without any apprehension, within point blank shot, though nothing would have induced me to place myself within his reach. We both took deliberate aim and fired : and perceived by his motions that we had given him rather a serious wound, though both of us were so ignorant of the animal that we fired at parts of the body almost at a venture. He seemed to be in a passion, raising his great upper jaw, showing his teeth and occasionally turning over and over like a stuck hog. He endeavored to escape, and to reach the river, but was not able to get along without difficulty, and made little progress for an hour and a half, during which we were occupied in attempts to kill him. We struck him with fifteen or sixteen balls in succession, before he was so far disabled, that we were emboldened to approach him. We at last got a rope round him near the head, and found that he had lost blood, particularly from a hole in the neck made by the first shot. He measured sixteen feet, and had been a most formidable animal, though now, to all appearance, scarcely alive. We tied the rope fast to a heavy log, intending to preserve his skin : but on returning next morning were

11*

surprised to find the rope broken and the monster gone. A few days afterwards we found him dead in the river, with the remainder of the rope on his neck.

The potatoes planted here it was afterwards found, although they grew rapidly, were put into the ground too late. They should have been sown in February, instead of the end of March. They appeared to flourish remarkably well; but it was afterwards found, on digging them, that when they had grown about as large as a walnut, they started on a second growth, and were thus good for nothing. The northern corn, brought by the agents from the United States, grew so rapidly, that although it did not rise high, it put out ears near the ground, and promised to come speedily to maturity. But the husks burst open when it began to ripen, which exposed the ears to the black birds; and they would strip them half bare in a moment, and then eat the kernels at pleasure. To prevent the ravages of these birds, it is the custom of the farmers to break the stalk just below the ear with a blow of an iron bar, and then bend it downward, so that they cannot strip it, as they would have to pull upwards. The agents planted southern corn also, but never got any valuable return from it; for although there was no bursting, the birds seized it in the milk and made great havoc. It was remarkable that the field planted by the owner of the land, did not suffer, although separated from their's only by a cart path. This they were inclined to attribute to the fact that his was a little later; and their's being first attacked by the birds served them until the other was too old.

CHAPTER XV.

On the fourth of April, after spending three more
days at Anahuac, I set out again for the coast, in
the same manner, and with the same company as
before. We reached South Bay that evening, and
encamped again on the shore. Our only design
was now to await the arrival of the Climax from
New-York, which was reported to have been seen
below, and as it was to bring out settlers for the
Company, would doubtless bring out letters also,
with instructions.

From the point where we were, we were not able
in the morning to ascertain our position so exactly,
as to decide how far we were from the shore of the
Gulf: for the Prairie which stretched away to the
south appeared to us to meet the sky. We therefore
sailed along the shore towards Point Bolivar, but
had not proceeded far, when we perceived something
beyond the land in that direction, which we were
confident must be the masts of a vessel; and draw-

ing up our boat where it would be out of the reach
of the water, we set off on foot across the Prairie,
to ascertain more about it. We found several marshes, and ponds or creeks, which intercepted our course,
and, in seeking to get round them, we at length got
separated from each other about a mile. We had
not very far to go however before we discovered the
Gulf of Mexico, full before us, and ascertained that
we had walked across Point Bolivar, the eastern cape
of Galveston Bay. Galveston Island, which lies
just off its mouth, stretched along on our right, and
nearly in front of us, and just within its eastern
point, we saw a schooner which appeared to lie upon
a shoal. On the beach we perceived a gentleman
and lady, with no attendant and no boat, and were
at a loss to imagine how they came there.

One of my companions joined them before I came
up, and when I approached introduced them as Mr.
and Mrs. Burnet, from New Jersey, who having
come out to settle on the San Jacinto, in the schooner
Cull, had run on the bar the preceding night, and
had just been landed by the Captain, who had gone
back to the vessel for more of the passengers. From
the account they gave us of the situation of the
vessel, we were filled with the greatest anxiety for
the persons still on board, who were apprehensive
that she would go to pieces in half an hour, and long
before they could be got on shore, as they had lost
their oars, and the boat could not land more than

two at a time.   When Mr. Burnet came off, the
people were throwing every thing overboard they
could lay their hands on, and considered themselves
in a most desperate situation.   We now felt that our
presence at that place with our boat was most fortunate; and without delay made our way back again
across the point, launched her, and rowed with all
speed two or three miles to the end of Point Bolivar.

We had supposed that we might be able with due
exertion to reach the vessel in an hour's time: but
as soon as we turned the point, we found the force
of the wind against us so great, that we could not
make any considerable progress, until two of us took
the painter and dragged it by walking in the surf,
leaving one of our number to steer.   This was
severe and unpleasant labor, and we made far less
speed than we wished, as we feared that delay might
be death to those in the schooner.   The beach is
smooth and uniform, and not encumbered with
rocks: for the whole southern region of Texas is
entirely destitute of stones—even of pebbles; but
yet the incessant rolling in of the swell from the
gulf rendered our progress very difficult, and we were
unable to go out beyond the breaking of the surf,
on account of the greater depth of water.   The news
we had come so far to obtain now appeared of no
moment, compared with the safety of so many of
our fellow creatures; and though Mr. B. had informed us that there were letters for us in the Cull, we

had lost all our impatience to obtain them. We saw articles of different descriptions floating here and there, which had been thrown overboard from the schooner, and particularly two large things like hogsheads, driving before the wind abreast of us up between Point Bolivar and the Island.

We thus labored two hours, when having got off against the schooner, we rowed out to her, and found that four or five of the passengers had already been landed by the Captain, but those remaining were still engaged in throwing overboard bricks, plank, &c. They soon desisted, however; and the wind and sea having somewhat subsided, the danger appeared less threatening. We refreshed ourselves on board; and having remained an hour or two, returned to the shore, landing not far from the Point. We chose a spot where most of the things thrown from the schooner had been driven on the beach; and immediately began to raise a shelter under which we might sleep in comfort. This was necessary, as on the wide Prairie and the long sand beach there was nothing to be seen. We first drove a plank obliquely into the sand, and then, with some nails which had been brought from the Cull, fastened a number of boards to it side by side in an upright position. Then, by laying other boards from the tops of these to the ground, and boarding up the end towards the wind, we soon had a good shelter pre-

pared against the night air, the sun and the rain.
Few articles of convenience had been brought on
shore, either in the boats or by the waves. We had
to content ourselves with laying boards on the sand
to sleep upon, (which one of our number jocosely
named New-York feather beds,) and had nothing
to spread upon them but a blanket for each person.
Having completed our house and arranged the furniture, we observed something singular floating near
us in the water, and found to our satisfaction that it
was a tin coffee cup; and soon after found several tin
cups, kettles, &c. which had also been thrown overboard. Making a fire upon the beach, we invited our
new friends to partake of our poor hospitality, and soon
formed a supper party, and highly relished our coffee.
It was surprising to us all that we were able to sleep
soundly on such hard couches, and that we felt
greatly refreshed from all our fatigue when we woke
in the morning. What was particularly gratifying,
was that a lady, totally unaccustomed to hardships,
and thrown thus suddenly upon an inhospitable, and
but for us an uninhabited shore, in a country which
she had never before seen, should so soon recover her
strength after the indifferent accommodations afforded
by a mere hut upon the beach.

We had received our letters in the mean time;
and in one of mine I found one of the most beautiful
little pieces of scrip ever purchased. The design and

execution showed the skill of an artist; and I could not but compare its value with that of twenty thousand acres of land.

By the first light of morning we discovered with joy, that the schooner had got afloat in the night, and was now sailing prosperously along abreast of us towards the entrance of Galveston Bay. Our companions, therefore, bidding us a hasty adieu, put off to her in the boat, and left us to occupy ourselves as we might in that lonely spot. It was a calm and pleasant day, and we sauntered about, wishing for the arrival of the Climax, a vessel preparing to sail for Galveston from New-York when I left there. The wind was so light during the day, that the Cull remained in sight till near night. Among the few incidents of the day, I may mention the appearance of a hog on the Prairie, to which we gave chase, hoping to obtain a supply of pork for our larder: but though we did our best to drive him towards the point with the hopes of getting a shot at him, after many races and doublings he got off and we lost him. We at first supposed the animal must have strayed from some farm at no great distance, as we still could not divest ourselves of the idea that such a country must be inhabited: but we afterwards found, that there was not a human being in any part of that region nearer than about eight miles; and the hog had probably been long running wild.

As evening approached we prepared our supper,

and were seated at it when we were surprised at the reappearance of one of the passengers of the Cull, who informed us that the schooner had again grounded, and lay in a dangerous situation a little way up Galveston Bay. The two agents of the Land Company immediately took the boat and proceeded again to the aid of the vessel, leaving us to reflect on the singular circumstances in which we were. The passengers of the Cull evidently placed great reliance upon us not only for assistance, but for advice, and were as ready to be guided by our opinions as if we had been pilots on that coast for years, while we were almost entirely ignorant of the sea, and had been thrown seasonably in their way only through our ignorance of the place. In the morning the Cull was again afloat, and making sail proceeded up the bay, towards the San Jacinto river, where, as I have before mentioned, Mr. Burnet had prepared to erect a steam saw mill.

I forgot to mention, that the objects which we had seen floating up the bay, and had mistaken for hogsheads, were the boilers intended for the mill. It was a little remarkable, that the manufacturer in New-York had declared, that, in case of shipwreck, they would be safe, as he had stopped and caulked them with care. Such an opportunity was now offered for an experiment. We afterwards learnt, that these great boilers, which were thrown overboard only to lighten the vessel, were driven by the wind along the coast up the entrance of the bay, and finally to its western shore, where they were afterwards found uninjured, after a chance voyage of about ten miles. They are now in Mr. Burnet's saw mill on the San Jacinto river.

The next day an event occurred which afforded us new occupation, and banished the recollection of the Cull and her concerns. We had observed a little pilot-boat built schooner making towards the bay from the eastward, and after she had got within the shelter of the island, we had a visit from the Captain, who had discovered our habitation, and come on shore to spend the night. We invited him into our dwelling, and learnt that he had chartered his vessel in New Orleans, for two hundred dollars, to two Frenchmen who were passengers on board, and were going to Anahuac with a load of coffee, whiskey and claret. Just off the island they had fallen in with a clumsy boat belonging to Colonel Bradburn, which he had sent, with a captain and four Mexican soldiers, to Brazos river, to see about cutting timber. As their boat was a dull sailer, they had got on board the schooner.

I woke in the night quite indisposed, and heard the wind blowing violently and the roar of the sea. When the light permitted, we discovered the masts of the schooner only above the water, which was very rough, with a signal of distress flying at half-mast, and nothing of the hull visible except a mere corner

of the deck. Our apprehensions were naturally
excited for those on board; but it was evidently
impossible to afford them any relief in so high a sea.
We were therefore obliged to content ourselves with
looking on; and thus we spent several hours gazing
at the vessel in her forlorn condition, being just able
now and then to perceive some of the men, apparently engaged at work.

It was perfectly evident that there was no possi-
bility of rendering any assistance to the vessel under
present circumstances, or even of obtaining any
information concerning the condition of the crew
beyond what we possessed. My companions therefore sought occupation by a walk into the interior,
while I remained in the hut, suffering under the
symptoms of fever. I betook myself to my hard
bed, and after listening a while to the incessant roar
of the winds and waves fell asleep. After some
time I started from sleep with a belief that the building was on fire, and felt much of the wild agitation
of a feverish dream, it being some time before I could
convince myself that every thing was safe, and
realize with distinctness recent events which had
occurred in that solitary place, on the margin of the
Gulf of Mexico, which was still roaring as before,
and dashing against the shores and the feeble little
vessel, which appeared to retain its former position.
The idea of fire, which at first so strongly impressed
me, I think may have arisen from the flapping of a

corner of my red silk handkerchief in the air, as it blew near my face as I lay; for it fluttered about like flames blown by the wind.

Feeling revived by the air, I sought my friends, whom I found catching crabs in a bayou not far off; and having a keen appetite I joined them in eating a large quantity. Kindling a fire and putting them into a boiling pot, we had a highly relished feast; which seemed to restore me to health, as my unfavorable symptoms gradually disappeared.

The wind and waves having somewhat subsided about two o'clock, the Captain, accompanied by one of our companions, in our boat, visited the vessel; but they found those on board so anxious to land, that they kept at a distance awhile deliberating what to do. The situation of the schooner was worse than we had apprehended. She had sprung aleak in the night and sunk on the bar as low as she could go down, leaving only a corner of her quarter deck above board; and the boat had been stove, so that the men had now been for many hours in the water up to their middles, and were much exhausted. As the boat could hold but four; the Captain insisted that the crew should promise to place in it only the two weakest. This was agreed to; and they selected the two Frenchmen, owners of the cargo, one of whom was helpless, and had to be lifted in. We were anxiously waiting for them on their arrival, and much commiserated the unfortunate strangers,

12*

who were consigned to our care under such painful circumstances. One of them could but just utter a few words, while the other was so far exhausted, that he could neither speak nor stand. The boat immediately returned to the vessel, while the three of us who remained took the poor men up to our habitation, wrapped them in blankets, administered a little whiskey, laid them down near the fire, and rubbed them briskly to quicken the circulation. They soon began to feel better, and in two hours were nearly restored. It was affecting to see their expressions of gratitude, which they made by all the means in their power: our ignorance of their language not allowing much intelligible conversation.

Before they were quite well the boat came ashore again, rowed by the mate of the schooner, who appeared strong and active, and brought two or three persons with him. After standing a little while by our fire, however, much to our surprise, he began to lose his strength, and was unable to make any exertion, though not at first conscious of it himself. He wished to return with the boat, to aid those still remaining on board, but found himself unable to hold an oar. In a short time his condition gave us serious alarm, and we tried to keep him up by exercise, taking turns with each other in running with him by holding him up, for about an hour. We had learnt that soon after the accident, the crew, having got at a demijohn of whiskey, made such free use of it that it was exhausted in the course of the forenoon. To this and the want of food we attributed their extreme exhaustion since the supply had failed.

The boats brought on shore two at a time until all were landed. The Captain of the Mexicans and one of his soldiers were so far gone when they landed that they were quite speechless; but under our treatment they were gradually restored to strength. We had now a large family to provide for; and though it was a light task to feed four, our number being now fifteen, it required forethought. Happily we were well supplied with several kinds of food in considerable quantities, viz: flour, pork, and coffee, and could obtain oysters and crabs to any amount by a little labor, while the birds on the Prairie might be had for the shooting. We set the Mexicans to making bread, to see how well they understood it, that we might learn something from them; but found that the method I had proposed, though I had never tried it, would prove more to our taste. They made very thin cakes of flour and water, and laid them among the coals without regard to cleanliness; and these, with claret and whiskey for some and coffee for others, formed our supper.

In the morning we found that the schooner retained her position. I undertook to make bread, and by getting some fat from a bit of pork which I melted in the frying pan, mixing it with flour and

water, and baking rolls in the same utensil, succeeded to my wishes. The sea being now calm, four
or five of us rowed off in one of the boats to the
vessel; and after opening the hatches, got out as
much of the cargo as we could take to the land.
We got out fifteen or twenty casks of whiskey,
which we towed ashore, and took in the boat about
the same number of bags of damaged coffee, hooked
up from the cabin some of the Frenchmen's clothes,
and took off the sails and rigging, and a few other
articles of different descriptions. At the close of day
we had done a good deal of work, and provided ourselves with a considerable amount of goods such as
they were.

CHAPTER XVI.

WE could now reflect at our leisure upon the unexpected circumstances in which we were placed. We had engaged but a few days before in an excursion of pleasure, after very little deliberation, taking a scanty supply of provisions, and thinking it very probable that we might meet no one before our return to Anahuac, or see any thing of particular interest. The most interesting occurrence we had anticipated, was the safe arrival of one of the expected vessels, with letters from our correspondents. Now, we had already passed through several trying scenes, had contributed to the preservation of several lives, had the care of a large number of strangers thrown upon us, and had obtained possession of a quantity of goods, most of which we might have claimed as our own for salvage. Indeed we were like the lords of the territory, might exercise the rights of property over the land and its productions, and demand tribute of the sea; for there was no previous competitor, and our companions were so grateful for our services, as to yield to our wishes in every thing.

The next day, having little to occupy us, and wishing to keep our hands busy, we undertook to raise a flagstaff, to attract the attention of the Climax, or any other vessels which might arrive, and enable them to discover the entrance of the bay, so difficult to recognize from sea. We had found a spar forty feet in length which had been driven on shore; and having drawn it up near our hut, nailed a board on to lengthen it, and decorated this with a piece of white cloth taken from the vessel, and several red kandkerchiefs so arranged as to bear some resemblance to a flag. Having attached to it a lanyard, with some difficulty we raised it, and planted it firmly in the ground. We subsequently paid several visits to the vessel, whence we brought a small American flag, which was afterwards substituted for the former.

The snipe, plover, and ducks, which abounded near us, afforded a considerable article of food; and birds of several other species we sometimes added to the number. One day we were supplied with a large addition, by a high tide, which rose over a small hollow, and on retiring left a great many little fish, about eight inches in length, which were well flavored.

We had thus abundance of game on different sides of us. As for deer, although we often saw

them on the Prairie, and though they sometimes
started from the grass and ran off as we passed
along without our guns, we knew too well their
piercing sight and rapid movements to pursue them.
It would be difficult for a person who has never
seen a great abundance of water fowl, to imagine
how innumerable they appeared to us at this place.
Immense flocks were ever to be seen floating on the
bayous and filling the air above them; and so
unaccustomed were they to the interference of men,
that we easily shot a plenty of them every day.
Gulls in great multitudes were perpetually to be
seen.

But what peculiarly attracted my attention and
often excited my astonishment, were the flocks of
pelicans which abounded along the shores. Such
novelties to a northerner, do not soon lose their
singularity in his eyes. These fowl are very
gregarious, always assembling together, and generally were to be seen in great numbers. There
are two species, which kept almost entirely separate,
the white and the grey. The spot on which we
had built our hut was a few yards from a part of
the shore, which I concluded had been their favorite
resort. There they assembled in great numbers for
several days after our arrival, and seemed to leave
it with reluctance. Each flock appeared to have a
leading bird, to which the rest paid voluntary respect,
so far as to follow him wherever he chose to lead,

walking in a single file, like a flock of geese. I
presume I have seen a thousand together, ranged
for half a mile along the beach. Being by no
means a very timid fowl, and quite heavy in flying,
it was not difficult to get a fair shot at them; but
it was long before either of us was able to bring one
down; and we never killed a second. We probably
had fired nearly an hundred times without effect:
the shot, as I suppose, glancing from the strong
feathers, for all our guns were for small shot, except
one rifle. The pelican which was killed, was shot
through the head, and had a large quantity of fish
in his pouch, which would hold, I suppose about a
gallon. These birds also abound on Pelican
Island, which lies a little up Galveston Bay.

I was roaming one morning without my fowling
piece, along the beach, when there was quite a thick
fog; and after passing a large quantity of the dry
drift wood which was scattered along the sand,
being brought from the Mississippi by the waves,
I found myself near a multitude of birds of different
kinds, chiefly gulls. To my surprise they did not
fly; and though I approached to within a very
short distance of them, perhaps three or four yards,
they did not appear to see me, and continued to
feed with the greatest unconcern. From the observations I then had an opportunity to make, I
argued that their vision was inferior to my own
under those circumstances. Whether it was owing

to the fog or not I can only conjecture; but the difference between our sight was just about the same as that between of a Trustee of a Land Company, and a purchaser of scrip.

Being as yet ignorant of the fate of Mr. Burnet's large steam boilers, since they had floated by us on the first day of our arrival, we paid a visit to Pelican Island, to see whether they had gone on shore there or not. It is two or three miles long, and abounds in birds, particularly pelicans: but we found no traces of what we were in search of, and returned.

We had hoped our flagstaff might serve as a landmark to the Climax, in case she should again appear off the coast; for having sailed by, as was reported, without discovering the passage, we had reason to expect her soon back again. The low and uniform appearance of the whole coast, including that of Galveston Island, renders it almost impossible to ascertain the position of a vessel at any considerable distance from the land. A day or two after our flag had been raised, the expected vessel reappeared. Discovering that she was off an inlet, though without perceiving our signal, she sent her boat with five men to examine the shore, who, observing our flag after they had gone some distance, steered for it, and landed about an hour before sunset on the beach near our hut. We made them welcome, and learnt from them with greater

13

certainty, every thing concerning the vessel. As we knew the entrance into the bay, one of our party set off to board her, after a little delay, with the sailors in their boat ; but this was a very imprudent step, as what took place might have been foreseen. The Climax, not seeing the boat, and for fear of the close neighborhood of the land, stood off a little; and it was not long before it became so dark, that we lost sight of both boat and vessel. It seemed inevitable that the six men must spend the night on the water, and this gave us much concern, as we knew they were unprovided, having nothing to eat, and only a jug of whiskey to drink. During the night the wind rose, and soon increased in violence, till we had a gale, though much less severe than what we had witnessed on the coast.

It was not, however, until about three o'clock the next day, that we obtained any information of their fate. We then discovered our companion walking up the shore from the eastward, and learnt from him, that he had been exposed in the open boat all night on the water, had had nothing to eat, had just finished a fatiguing walk of three hours on the level beach, having landed, as he supposed, about fifteen miles from us. After losing sight of the vessel the evening before, the men had headed the boat, as they supposed, for the land, drank whiskey, and lay down ; but in the morning could see neither vessel nor land. At length, some hours after, they discovered the shore, and on reaching it were entirely at a loss to determine whether they were on the main land or on Galveston Island, which excited their lively anxiety, because on the latter, they feared no food could be obtained. Not long afterwards, however, the vessel appeared in sight, and he thought he could recognize some of the logs of drift wood on the beach, though in this he must have been mistaken. He therefore proceeded for home on foot, while the sailors remained by the boat.

Having furnished him with necessary refreshments, on looking to sea about an hour afterwards, the vessel was discovered again. We then launched our boat and proceeded some distance towards her with our sail, when seeing her tack to stand off, and knowing we should have but little time to sail before it would be dark, we reflected on the warnings we had had against pursuing ships at night, and put back. We then perceived that the Climax had come to anchor.

That night the wind began to blow with violence, and we soon had a far more severe gale than any we had before experienced on the coast. We awoke occasionally during the night, sufficiently to realize that the storm was terrible, and the sea most violently agitated : but knowing that we had nothing to do, aud thinking we had nothing to fear, it did not long interrupt our slumbers. In the morning,

however, on leaving our hut, we found the sea had
risen above the highest tides we had witnessed, by
three or four feet, and almost reached our door.
The sandy beach was in some places covered by
the waves, which rolled and dashed violently quite
up into the green grass around us, which formed
the margin of the beautiful Prairie. At the same
time the rain was falling copiously, and every thing
seemed ready to melt into the one great fluid element.
The wind had been thus blowing directly on shore
for several hours; and we naturally concluded, when
we contemplated the scene, and considered the force
of the storm, that the ship must have been inevitably
wrecked.

CHAPTER XVII.

FULLY impressed with the idea that the brig must
have been wrecked, and wishing to afford aid to
any of the crew, as well as to relieve our own lively
anxiety, without waiting to take food, in a heavy
rain, we set off about break of day on an excursion along the coast to the eastward, presuming
from the direction of the wind, that if any thing
had been driven on shore from the vessel, we should
find it. We walked fast, and before we slackened
our pace, must have got a considerable distance
from home, but yet found nothing. We began at
length to think our fears might perhaps prove ground-
less, when we discovered a barrel on the beach
before us, and within a short distance a box of
bottled cider and two strings of onions. The barrel,
we found, was filled with vinegar; and the box we
soon found means to open, being quite thirsty with
our rapid march. I can say, that few draughts I
ever took proved more grateful, than such a fine

13*

beverage under those circumstances. The idea of the vessel's loss, made us press on again with renewed vigor; and as we proceeded we found several other light articles on the shore, such as tables, chairs, &c., which had evidently been thrown overboard. The thickness of the air, however, did not permit us to see far before us. At length, when we had walked about four miles from our hut, and it had become broad daylight, we perceived the vessel very near us, at first hardly discernible through the mist, sitting upright upon the beach, and driven almost up to the grass of the Prairie; her masts gone, but her hull apparently safe and sound. The sea was still very rough, and she was surrounded by water, as the waves ran up a little beyond her: but we concluded at once, that she was too high to be in any manner affected by them, as we had walked dry-shod, the day before, along the beach exactly where she lay. We soon perceived the men on board, actively engaged in throwing articles of different kinds into the water; and their consternation appeared to us so unreasonable, that there was something almost ludicrous in it. On discovering us they expressed great surprise and gratification; but the tumult of the water made it very difficult to hear each other's voices. They could not at first be convinced by our signs that they were in a state of perfect safety. We called to them that they were on the main land, on the borders of a rich country, and not very far from our temporary habitation, hoping they would take a little courage; but they could not distinctly hear us. We proposed to them to launch their boat, which we saw had been preserved; but found they were afraid to trust it in the waves, which were indeed rushing up and down around the vessel with considerable force.

To show them how shallow the water was, I walked into it, intending to wade up to the vessel, which was not now more than ten rods from us. After a few steps, what was my surprise to find I had no footing! I sunk in an instant into deep water, head and ears, and had to swim for my life; and though I was soon safely back again on the sand, was wetter than before. The beach being a quick sand, the currents caused by the obstruction presented by the hull had cut a deep channel on each side of her, and the vessel's weight had been gradually crowding out the sand from beneath her, till she had sunk and imbedded herself to a considerable depth. This operation, so familiarly known to seamen under similar circumstances, I was ignorant of before: but though unfavorable to a vessel's getting off again when thrown upon the sand, it often secures the lives of crews and passengers. At length they were prevailed upon to launch their boat; and when they were informed of their situation, they became quite calm, and began to land their passengers, of

whom there were thirty or forty, who had come to
settle in Texas.

From the darkness, the thickness of the weather,
and their ignorance of the coast, the Captain had
been under an apprehension that he was on a shoal,
(for he had not been able to see the land distinctly,)
and had been throwing things overboard for three or
four hours.   We did what we could to aid the landing of the passengers, taking the women and children
first; and worked in the water for a full hour.
Having at length seen them all on shore, and finding
we could be of no further service immediately, we
proposed to return home to breakfast.   The Captain
had informed us that his vessel had sprung aleak,
and the water was in the cabin.   This, added to her
position, convinced us that she was lost, and therefore there remained but one course to be pursued,
which we told them they must adopt without delay.
This was to build a large hut on the land, make
themselves as comfortable as possible, and take such
measures as they could to get to Anahuac, whither
they were bound.

We returned home tired and hungry, taking in
our way the remains of the cider, the onions, and a
bottle of vinegar, which, added to our breakfast, (or
rather dinner,) of raw salt pork were highly relished
on arriving at our hut, about noon, after fasting all
the morning.   In a short time we set off again for

the wreck, leaving the Mexicans and Frenchmen, as we thought they could do no good, and they were very obedient to all our directions.

Happily there were among the passengers in the vessel two very good carpenters, whose services proved highly important in constructing a habitation, while materials were obtained in abundance, from those brought out for the erection of buildings. We rendered them what assistance we could; and they soon had pitched several tents, made of sails; and producing such provisions, utensils, &c. as they could conveniently come at, began to find themselves in a situation comparatively comfortable. The ship's cook, a large negro, was particularly active during the day, for abstinence and fatigue had rendered his vocation doubly important. This fellow, who was strong and quite skillful in his profession, bore the name of General Midnight, and sometimes rendered us also obliging services. On our return home at night, we took with us several men who had no accommodations as yet provided for them; and in the morning, according to arrangements made with the Captain, furnished several barrels of flour and some other articles which we had saved from the New Orleans vessel, in exchange for objects more in demand with us.

The poor Frenchmen, whose property they had been, seemed rather sorrowful as we rolled the barrels to the boat, but I must do them the justice to

say, that they offered no objection. They must
have realized the circumstances in which we were
placed. In the first place, they doubtless owed us
their lives; then, it was to be recollected, we had a
legal claim to most of the property for salvage; and
thirdly, after having done all in our power for their
comfort, by sharing house and food with them, necessity required a sacrifice of some of the remaining
goods for things of which we all stood in equal
need.

Things went on well at the wreck, and, every
visit we paid to the spot, we found some new improvement. All were anxious to remove as soon as
possible: but as yet it was difficult to fix on any
plan likely to be soon carried into effect. Finding
how skillful the carpenters were, and having ascertained that they were boat-builders also, I recommended to them the construction of a boat to transport
themselves to Anahuac with their tools, which were
very valuable. I was confident that no other means
could be obtained without expense, and that the
boat would command a good price at any time.
Among these unfortunate people, thus cast on shore
in a strange land, I had every day occasion to reflect
on the advantages of a practical education. Here
was a body of men almost entirely dependant for
their comfort on two of their number, though some of
them perhaps had been trained in early life in a more
expensive manner, and with superior expectations.

Actively engaged, and sensible of rendering themselves useful, these two were among the happiest of the entire company, while they enjoyed the gratification of knowing, that they should find abundant and profitable employment at the first settlement they might reach.

CHAPTER XVIII.

Point Bolivar, (*Continued.*)—Messengers from Anahuac to learn our fate.—Return thither.—A night on Bird Island.—Singular shrubs.—Birds, nests, eggs, a random shot.—Point Bolivar.

We had now been a fortnight on the coast, during which we had such constant and varied occupation as scarcely to think of Anahuac, or of what conclusions our friends there would be likely to form concerning the cause of our absence. We had proposed but a short excursion of two or three days at the utmost, and they knew that our provision was small, and our boat frail. If we had reflected, we might have presumed that their anxiety would be highly excited. But we did not reflect on the subject; and were at first much surprised when we saw, three or four days after the wreck of the Climax, two boats arrive at our habitation, with several men from Anahuac, who had come with long faces to inquire after us, well persuaded that we had perished in the bay of Galveston, or the Gulf of Mexico, where they supposed we had been exposed in sounding the channel. They met us with joy, and we received them with astonishment, until we began to reflect, when their anxiety appeared both natural and friendly.

One of the boats belonged to the Land Company, and the other to Colonel Bradburn—a flat vessel, which he had built in the province, and sent down under command of one of Lafitte's old pirates.

The appearance of the boats from the interior was gratifying to the colony on the coast below us: but they soon realized that they would have to pay a high price for a conveyance to Anahuac: Col. Bradburn proposing to charge for the freight of articles from the wreck twice as much as they paid for bringing them from New-York. The carpenters found that the advice they had followed was very good: for they had begun to build a boat of materials partly picked up on the beach, and partly taken from the vessel. They had shown every disposition to be guided by my opinion: for they had brought out letters to me, and knew that I had some knowledge of the country, while they had none.

That day we were served with a feast of peculiar delicacy: for having been out with our guns, we had obtained a great number of birds and water fowl, and committing them to the care of General Midnight, they made a fine addition to the simple food which the stores afforded. The people around us, newly arrived in that fertile country, viewed the abundant game on the Prairies with as much surprise as we had done, and considered it a great feat to kill two or three brace of ducks in the course of a morning ramble, while to us it was rather a piece of

14

condescension to spend our powder on them. The colonists, who during the storm had regarded the coast on which they were thrown with so much apprehension, had been so much struck with admiration at the appearance of fertility and beauty in the landscape around them, that they had contemplated making a settlement somewhere near the spot where they had pitched their tents: but the account they now heard from our visiters made them relinquish this idea, and turned all their attention to other subjects.

Thinking we were in some measure bound to relieve the anxiety of our friends at Anahuac, I set off the next morning, with the Captain of the Climax in his boat, as he was going to make arrangements for the sale of the wreck and cargo, being uncertain whether they were insured or not. We were accompanied by one of the boats which had come down, and had a prosperous passage of sixty miles to Anahuac. There I met with Mr. Heyne, (whose house I had visited before, as the reader will recollect;) and as he wished to purchase a sail for his boat which he had brought with him from Old River, he invited me to return with him to Point Bolivar, which I cheerfully acceded to.

On our way down Galveston Bay, as night approached, we found ourselves near a small island which I had noticed on the passage up, on account of the remarkable number of birds which were

constantly flying over it. Mr. Heyne, who was well
acquainted with every spot in this region, proposed
to spend the night on the little island. The moon
was shining bright when we approached it, and I
observed that it was overgrown with shrubbery,
intermingled with prickly pears, about six feet high.
The croaking and other notes of birds convinced me
that the island was no less a roosting place by night
than a resort by day. My older companion, with all
the familiarity of experience, immediately began to
prepare for supper, assisted by his son, about nineteen
years of age, whom I did not mention before ; while
I took the old man's gun, which was very long, and
walked round to the opposite side of the land.
There I was astonished to find a multitude of fowl,
generally white, roosting on the shrubbery, so thickly
standing side by side, that it seemed almost like a bank
of snow. After observing them for a time, as closely
as the moonlight would allow, I discharged my heavy
loaded old gun into the midst of them, thinking I
might thus easily secure an abundant breakfast for
our little party. But the confusion with which I
thus surrounded myself perfectly dismayed me
Hundreds, indeed I think I might say thousands of
birds instantly flew up, with such a fluttering, and
screaming, and yelling, that no scene of noise and
hubbub I ever witnessed could be at all compared
with it. I was now in the very midst of such a
crowd of fowls as I had before only seen from a dis

tance; and they must have their organs of hearing very differently hung or regulated from mine, or they never could put up with the company of each other. After I had recovered from the first stunning caused by their unspeakable din and confusion, I began to leave the spot, and was glad to find myself soon in the company I had left, and to hear their voices at some little distance, as they gradually ceased their various notes, and began to settle again upon their roosts.

Our supper was already on the highway of preparation, under the care of Mr. Heyne, who was making the best use of the materials at his command, and soon presented me with one of those fine cups of coffee which I almost invariably met with in Texas. Drawing up and turning over our boat, spreading our blankets upon the ground, and wrapping ourselves in our cloaks, we then lay down; and the birds and ourselves, I believe, were silenced by a sound sleep in as short a time as I have taken to tell of it. As usual in those times, I scarcely waked at all until early morning, and then rose refreshed and in fine spirits. Not doubting that the old gun had done some execution on the preceding evening, I determined to pay a visit to the spot: but I found objects of wonder before I arrived at it.

I now perceived, on looking more closely around me, that the little island, which had a loose, stony, sandy soil, was almost covered with bushes about six feet in height, which grew so thick as to be often impenetrable by man, though abounding with birds of different kinds, which traversed the ground beneath with great freedom. The most animated scene surrounded me: for wherever I went and on whatever side I looked, every bush and almost every twig seemed to be occupied by feathered tenants of some size and description or other. On reaching the spot where I had fired into the bushes the evening previous, I was not surprised to find that my shot had taken effect: but I was astonished to see about twenty water fowl lying dead upon the ground. These were generally birds of considerable size, though some of them possessed only superior longitude: for among those I picked up were bodies not bigger than a small duck's mounted on legs measuring a foot and a half below the knee. Almost all of them had plumage abundant and white, or bordering on pink, and necks long enough to keep up a connexion with the earth. I showed my prizes to my experienced companion, who immediately condemned the whole lot as good for absolutely nothing; and they were of course rejected.

We proceeded a little further among the bushes, when we found the birds multiplied beyond any thing I had ever imagined. Their nests were placed so near as almost to touch each other, the ground was half covered with eggs of different colors and sizes, which had fallen out; and the chattering

14*

every where was almost deafening. There was something peculiar in the growth of the bushes, which were generally of an uniform height, and at once so flat on the top and so strong, that after getting up I could walk upon them for several rods, six feet from the ground. There were multitudes more of nests to be seen, built side by side, while on the interior and lower boughs every spot seemed occupied which was capable of sustaining the habitation of a large bird or a small one. Notwithstanding the confusion of sounds, of arrangements and of occupations among those busy creatures, no collision seemed to take place in business, and no jealousies were betrayed by neighbors. My comrade explained the reason for so many eggs being found on the sand, by telling me that the season of hatching had been for some time past. This was confirmed by the abundance of young fowl every where to be seen on the ground, and in many of the nests, as well as by the worthlessness of the few first eggs which we gathered and broke. The variety of appearance among the birds was increased by the number of young ones, some of which were very unlike the parents, and others seemed to be of double their size. In some instances a chick or two would be seen, too young or too lazy to take care of themselves, yet filling alone brim-full a nest as large as a crow's, before they had ever left home.

Mr. Heyne began to collect some of the eggs,

saying he could distinguish the good ones, and had soon gathered several hatfulls, which we took to the boat. Most of these were of good size, but those we saw varied from the size of a robin's egg to that of a duck's.

On arriving at Point Bolivar we found all well; and on proceeding to the wreck learnt that arrangements were nearly made for selling the vessel and cargo at auction. The various articles of merchandise, sails, rigging, furniture, &c. were collected in lots; and the sale at length commenced: several persons from Anahuac, and some of the passengers appearing as purchasers. The prices were, on the whole, about as favorable as could have been expected under such circumstances.

Here we now found ourselves, surrounded by more companions in misfortune. The emigrants in the Climax, whose arrival had been apprehended rather than desired, under existing circumstances, had now come, to experience the overthrow of all their hopes, and to add to the inconveniences and trials of those who had preceded them. It was painful to witness their disappointment in learning the state of things, now so familiar to ourselves; and to anticipate what lay before them. The general agent of the Land Company had come in the Climax; and on learning the facts made up his mind to return to the United States. This object he effected in a vessel which offered him a passage a few days after his arrival, while the other agents were left to render the new emigrants as comfortable as they could.

The carpenters now found their prospects among the brightest of all the passengers. They had completed their boat in two days, but it was so strong and large that they transported several passengers to Anahuac in it, beside carrying all their own property. On our arrival there, they applied to me to find them a purchaser for it; and my old comrade, Mr. Heyne, was glad to get it for fifty dollars. Their skill was soon in high demand: for in that country, where land is so cheap and productive, the climate so favorable and game so abundant, men soon lose the disposition for labor, and workmen of all kinds are generally very scarce. The agents of the Land Company now needed temporary accommodations for the settlers who had come in the Climax; and the carpenters were soon at work, building shanties on contract, and in as good spirits as any men I ever saw. And so successful were they, with other jobs also, that in two months they made about six hundred dollars.

CHAPTER XIX.

As we approached Anahuac, we discovered many of the inhabitants assembled on the shore, awaiting our arrival: it being a rare thing to witness such a sight as we presented with our new boat, which had been named the Economist's Resource, with sails set and flag flying. When we landed, they saluted us with three cheers, and received us with other expressions of welcome.

One of the first things I did, was to inquire after my horse, which had been indulged with a long vacation, with those of my companions, on the wide and beautiful Prairie. I was informed that one of our friends had been out, caught and rode him on one occasion, but that he had set every other attempt to take him, in other cases, entirely at defiance, although encumbered with his hobble, which a person unaccustomed to seeing horses so confined, would have supposed must have materially checked his speed. I took a walk upon the Prairie, to see whether I could recapture the wild and trickish little spirit, by any device or exertion.

The Prairie looked much more green and fertile than when I had travelled upon it in coming from the Brazos, the grass had been growing, and the leaves thickening their foliage during the fortnight which had elapsed; and the variety presented by the groves, points, and islands of wood, affording a new aspect on almost every side to which I turned, was remarkably rich and agreeable. It did not seem at all surprising, that a horse, turned out for two weeks, on so extensive and fine a pasture, after performing a journey, though neither long nor wearisome, should be unwilling to resign his freedom; and when I discovered my mustang at a distance, I perceived that he had become as much accustomed to that mode of life, as I had to living on the seacoast. He moved with freedom and considerable rapidity by long springs, which was the only manner in which his confinement allowed him to go; and this singular gait, which I had not seen for some time, again excited my risibility, though I expected it to prove the cause of great vexation to me, for I saw not how I should be able to overtake the animal if he felt, as I presumed, in the humor for a race. Much to my gratification, however, on perceiving me, he stood still, and watched me closely for a little time, and then began to approach, evidently recognizing me, and recollecting, as I suppose, my old flapped hat, which he had been accustomed to, and which I still wore.

On reaching the village, I took him to a blacksmith to be shod; but the man was half drunk, and so much afraid of the little horse, which had a wilder look than usual, and seemed all the time ready to play some trick or other, that he stood off, and would not come near enough so much as to handle his feet. Even after I had confined his head by twisting his nose with a wythe, the blacksmith still kept aloof; and could not be induced to attempt paring away his hoof, which had been partly broken, and greatly needed it. After cutting it away with my jack knife, I got his foot in a better condition, and then began to think of proceeding on our journey to the north-west.

On the 30th of April we left Anahuac for Brazoria, by the way we came, viz; round the north eastern corner of the bay of Galveston. The shallowness of this large sheet of water, particularly along the northern part, and at the mouths of the rivers which there fall into it, is much to be regretted, as it must greatly interfere with the convenience of settlers, and deny most of the advantages afforded by navigable waters, unless means should be found to cut through the bars. While we were at Anahuac, the Company's agents had often to suffer inconvenience from

the grounding of their boat in proceeding to and
from their farm.

When we reached the crossing place on the
Trinity river, we found that Mr. Heyne had cut
down the bank, so as to render the descent to the
shore convenient, and had his new boat, (that made
by the emigrant carpenters,) in use as a ferry boat.
We had therefore no trouble to apprehend from the
unwillingness of our horses to leave the bank : but
I felt some apprehensions about trouble of another
kind. I recollected the ferry at Brazoria ; and,
although my fears might be unfounded, I thought
I would neither confess nor disregard them. I
therefore requested the ferryman to take my bridle,
with as much apparent indifference as I could express,
which he readily did ; but as soon as he began to
pull upon it, my white mustang began to scowl and
leer upon him most maliciously, and giving a sudden
spring flew at him like lightning, as if he had intended to kill him on the spot. The old colonist had
seen too many mustangs to keep his eye off from
him for a moment in such a case : (for I learnt that
this was by no means an uncommon trick among
the Texas horses,) but stepping aside just in time to
save his life : " You little witch, you !" he exclaimed,
as the animal lighted like a fury on the very place
where he had stood ; while I had difficulty in sup-
pressing laughter, equally amused at the tricks of
the one, and the coolness and circumspection of the
other.

On reaching Mr. Heyne's house, we discovered some other travellers a considerable distance before us : so stopping only to get a draught of milk, we hastened on, and overtaking them, joined their company. We had intended to spend the night at Winfrey's ; and found with pleasure that he was of the party. We had to pass, as before, by the singular route through a part of Galveston Bay : but our companions being familiar with it, we felt no apprehension, and encountered no difficulty.

We had afterwards to pass over another beautiful Prairie region, where our eyes were refreshed with the luxuriant scene presented on every side. The grass was nearly up to the horses' knees, and so thick and green, that it entirely concealed every trace of the black surface formed by the burning of the dry plants a few weeks preceding, and which was in some spots discernible when we passed this way before. In some places I observed patches covered with sensitive plants ; and in others flowers were blooming in great variety, while we were usually the only living objects to be seen. We saw occasionally the fine cattle belonging to the farms, ranging over their extensive estates ; but in the wide intervals between them, we seldom found any thing but the birds possessed of animal life. The cattle had already begun to show the effects of their improved pasturage, and were remarkably fat, sleek, and vigorous, ranging unrestrained over regions

immensely disproportioned even to their great numbers, and grazing to their hearts' content on herbage
which grew tenfold faster than they could consume
it. Here were shown, in a striking manner, evidences of the immeasurable resources of the country;
and it is not to be wondered at, by any person
acquainted with the nature of man, that he should
become indolent on a soil so ready to do all his labor
for him unassisted. We had been repeatedly told,
that industrious men might succeed in mechanic
arts to almost any extent, because there were none
in Texas to compete with them; and the two carpenters who came in the Climax, had excited much
astonishment by their activity at Anahuac. This
they might retain for a time; but a familiarity with
such scenes as we now witnessed would probably
soon dampen their zeal, and diminish their love of
labor.

At Mr. Winfrey's fine farm, and in his mansion,
so remarkable for its superior neatness and comforts,
we were again welcomed. His brother-in-law, Barrow, has an estate bordering upon his own.

CHAPTER XX.

THE next morning we were accompanied some distance on our way by our host, because he assured us we should need directions, particularly at one part of our route. Having before passed over it with a guide, we had not perceived any difficulty. Having proceeded some distance, and swum our horses across Cedar creek, which, as is common with the streams here, is bordered by a thick wood for the space of some rods on both sides, we found ourselves in a few minutes, on the verge of the broad Prairie beyond. From this spot, as Mr. Winfrey informed us, our route lay round the head of Goose Creek, a small tributary of the San Jacinto. Its course was marked by a distant line of woodland, extending some miles to the right, where it terminated. He told us that great care would be necessary, to avoid losing our way; and gave many directions, for which we thanked him, though we considered them almost unnecessary, because I had my pocket compass with me, and we had long been accustomed to steering by it both by land and water. The air was somewhat thick and misty, and the sky covered with clouds; so that much of the time we might be unable to see any of the distant groves or islands which were scattered here and there. There was, however, the point now in full view, and we had taken our direction on the compass; so bidding him good day on the borders of the wood, we proceeded somewhat carelessly over the verdant and boundless lawn that spread before us, in some places apparently to the horizon. What acres, what miles, what leagues square of the most fertile land were now in sight, without a human inhabitant! And how easy would it be for a stranger to become bewildered in travelling over them! There was not a road to be traced, not even the slightest appearance of a path, or of a single footstep. If any passenger had taken that course before this season, the rank herbage had entirely obliterated every evidence of it. An unbroken surface of grass, intermingled here and there with beautiful flowers, extended on every side of us to a great distance: in some places bounded by a distant grove or range of trees, and in others stretched far between points and islands of woodland till lost in the thickness of the air. These, however,

were often shut out from the view by the thickness
of the vapor, and there was nothing to vary the
scene, more than is found in the midst of the
ocean.

The idea of straying upon a Prairie for a long
time, had ere this presented itself to my imagination,
as a gloomy, and indeed a very dangerous and horrid
thing.   I had heard from different persons accounts
of such misfortunes, which made me apprehend the
loss of one's way as a very serious affair.   It is often
said of travellers on the Arabian deserts, and of
unfortunate mariners on a wreck, that thirst is the
most distressing evil they have to encounter.   And
this was fully confirmed by some of the tales I had
heard of wanderers on the Prairies of Texas.   Indeed I had listened to some, while passing over a
part of this same ground, on my way towards the
coast.   The young stranger who had then served as
our guide to Anahuac, had entertained me with
some of his own adventures of this nature.   I did
not mention him particularly before.   He was one
of those mysterious personages whom I met in
several places in Texas : men who had seen much,
and were ready to communicate freely on most
subjects, but always avoided every intimation concerning their own history.

The young man of whom I speak was about
twenty, evidently one of my own countrymen, and

15*

had received a pretty good education from teachers
or books, though a very indifferent one from his
parents or those with whom he had associated. He
had been in Texas two or three years, travelled in
every part of it, and was familiar with life and
manners, objects, places and circumstances in every
district. He was then on his way from the San
Jacinto, and had recently been lost on a Prairie.
Being alone one day, and travelling where there
were no landmarks, he became bewildered, and
sought in vain for any thing that might serve as a
guide. He was, I think, without a compass, and
directed his course wherever his judgement dictated,
riding on merely because his only hope was in
leaving the place where he was. He fortunately
had a small quantity of provisions with him, but
after these were gone, his principal fear was that his
tobacco would be exhausted before he should find his
way to some habitation : for being a great tobacco-
chewer, he thought it his only substitute for drink.
When night came he dismounted, confined his horse,
and slept on the Prairie. When morning returned,
he remounted and pursued his way.

According to my recollection, he had no gun with
him ; and this, I believe, was the reason why he
entertained no expectation of supplying himself with
food. After he had wandered, almost hopelessly, I
know not how long, to his great joy he struck a
track, where some person had previously passed on

horseback ; and quickening his pace, he pressed on,
hoping it might soon lead him to relief. He proceeded, however, hour after hour, and was about to
despair, when he was cheered by the discovery of
another track, which met and joined the one he
was pursuing. This restored his courage ; and
although it seemed strange that two travellers should
have joined company on such a vast and apparently
deserted Prairie, it was evident that the tracks had
been recently made, by horses moving at a travelling
gait, so that he could not doubt that such was the
fact, and that he was not far behind them.

He rode on again : but still nothing was to be seen
before him, except the level and open country. And
thus he spent several hours longer, wondering all the
while why he could not overtake the strangers, when
at length he perceived another grateful sign of man.
Another track, marked in the grass came up and
struck the route he was pursuing ; and now he had
the marks of three horses before him. Now once
more he spurred his horse, feeling as if company and
relief must be near. Three travellers, it would seem,
could hardly be travelling together after meeting in
this accidental manner, and all lost like himself :
some one of them at least, must have known the
way, it was reasonable to suppose ; and by following
their traces, he must undoubtedly, before long, arrive
at some habitation, or at least some stream. His
thirst, notwithstanding the tobacco he used, was

very distressing, and the hope of finding water was highly gratifying.

He had not, however, gone much farther, when he perceived something on the Prairie he thought he had seen before; and after a short examination and a little reflection, he concluded that he must have previously passed the spot. But how could this have occurred? He had not turned upon his track; but might he not have made a complete circle, while he had thought himself travelling in a straight course? Not only this might be true: but the truth suddenly flashed upon his mind—he had been following his own tracks for about two days! Having made one circuit, on striking his own route the first time, he had imagined it that of a stranger, and followed it with the most fallacious hopes, until he reached it again and again, in each instance mistaking the footsteps of his horse for those of another.

The wanderer had trials to undergo after this discouraging adventure, but nothing in his narrative had struck me so forcibly as this part of the story. Though he afterwards suffered more severely from hunger, and particularly from thirst, there was nothing which seemed to me so dreadful as his situation when he made the discovery of his long and useless wanderings round and round the Prairie in the same wide circle. He reached a habitation at length, and obtained water and food; but the latter part of his tale interested me comparatively little.

The recollection of such a tale was enough to make one feel a desire for water, and our ride had prepared us to relish a draught.

We had set out uncommonly early, that we might arrive at our intended lodging place, Mr. Lynch's on the San Jacinto, early in the afternoon : the distance being thirty miles. We travelled two or three hours, as we believed, directly towards the woody point indicated, and when we began to think we were near it, on the clearing away of the mist, it yet ap⁻ peared as distant as at first. After proceeding some time longer, and finding it still apparently retiring before us, we concluded that we had mistaken our landmark, or rather that our host had been deceived, for the error was too evident to be longer doubted. Observing another point of woods towards the left, we determined that there must be Goose Creek ; and changed our course in that direction. But on reaching the place after a long ride, we found, to our mortification, no appearance of a stream ; and nothing to indicate one in any direction. I went into the woods : but though I found some of the finest oaks, pines, and cedars I ever saw, some of the latter perhaps for sixty feet bare trunks, I discovered no water. On comparing our views too, we found them very contradictory ; so that when I proposed to proceed to the right, my companion insisted that we had erred in travelling too much in that direction, and strongly urged that we should go

to the left. The more we discussed the question
the more doubtful did we feel ; until we determined
to resort to the compass for direction : but what was
my mortification, on searching the pocket of my
round jacket, where I had put it, to find that it had
been dropped on the way, probably by the jolting of
the horse. The sky still continued to be over-clouded,
so that the sun's place could not be discovered : but
it was useless to remain where we were, and we
proceeded towards the left, and continued to ride,
though at best quite doubtful of our way.

I had never been at all prepared for the indescriba-
ble beauty of a Texas Prairie at this season of the
year, which I now could not avoid admiring, even
under such unpleasant circumstances.   The wild
flowers had greatly multiplied, so that they were
often spread around us in the utmost profusion, and
in wonderful variety.   Some of those which are
most cultivated in our northern gardens were here
in full bloom and perfection, intermingled with many
which I had never before seen, of different forms
and colors.   I should despair of giving my reader
any adequate idea of the scenes which were thus
so richly adorned, and through which we often passed for acres in extent, breaking for ourselves the
only path perceptible on the whole Prairie.   Among
the flowers were the largest and most delicate I had
ever seen, with others the most gaudy.   Among
them were conspicuous different species about six

inches in diameter, presenting concentric zones of the brightest yellow, red, and blue in striking contrasts. In more than one instance these fields of flowers were not only so gay and luxuriant as to seem like a vast garden richly stocked with the finest plants and abandoned to a congenial soil, but extensive almost beyond limitation : for it was sometimes difficult to discover whether they stopped short of the horizon. It was singular also that patches were here and there overspread by mimosas, which, as our horses passed through them, drew up their leaves and dropped their branches whenever they were brushed by their feet, thus making a withered trace on the surface, which was but gradually obliterated as these timid plants regained their courage, raised their stems again and expanded their withered leaves. The plants whose sensitiveness had thus been overcome, were rendered distinguishable to the eye from others, by the exposure they made of the lower side of their leaves when they folded them up : that side being of a much lighter hue than the upper. There was a phenomenon connected with this striking appearance, which I was at the time unable to account for, and could hardly credit. That was, the shrinking of the delicate plants a little in advance of us, before we had quite reached them. A friend who had witnessed the same thing, accounted for it by supposing that they received a shock through the long horizontal roots which connect them together.

One of the first flowers which appears to deck the Prairie in the spring, is the Prairie rose, which in blossom and fragrance resemble some of our rich red roses, though the shrub is quite different. As for others, I know not what a botanist might make of them : but I am certain that many of them would be exceedingly admired in our own country, as rich and new ; and as to the scenes over which they were spread, it is impossible to describe or to imagine their beauty and attraction.   After looking on the rich and ever varying display, I felt a high degree of pleasure and admiration, so that I thought I could almost give my mustang his liberty, throw myself on the ground and spend the whole season among them.   Occasionally too a light breath of wind would rise, and blow the mingled perfumes into my face, giving an enjoyment no less pure and refined, and most difficult to express.

Through these vast and splendid regions coursed occasionally a few deer.   We saw several herds of six or eight in the course of the day, and some much larger.   Most of them were accompanied by fawns, smooth, red and beautifully spotted, as innocent and frisky as young lambs, and like them keeping close to their dams wherever they went.   We found in this case as in others, that we might sometimes approach pretty near to them when we came against the wind, but they would scent us at a considerable distance from the leeward, and bound far away.   We

also saw several small droves of wild mustangs as
we travelled on, which betrayed greater interest or
curiosity towards us. They would start off at their
slow gallop, with their long mains and tails flying,
while their thick fetlocks and foretops gave them a
wild, untutored aspect; and sweeping off in a semi-
circle to the right or left, scour over half a mile or
a mile of the Prairie, and then stop to survey us
until we again approached them. After repeating
this manœuvre several times, they generally changed
their course and disappeared. These little horses
though not ill-formed, are destitute of the peculiar
beauty and elegance which are attributed to certain
wild species of larger size. They are also not very
swift: but yet are very valuable to the inhabitants,
and will doubtless long prove so.

These animals were gay and contented, because they were at home, on their native soil. We
on the contrary, were wandering in uncertainty, and
not without some danger of passing the night in
the open Prairie. About two o'clock, the clouds
so far cleared away as to show us the place of the
sun, which to our chagrin, we found on the wrong
side of us. We had now some evidence not only of
our error, but of the mode of correcting it; and turning our horses, we spurred them in the contrary
direction, and rode as fast as we thought they could
bear to travel, for an hour and a half or more, when
we reached a small stream, no doubt the creek we

16

had so long been in search of. Here we took a hearty draught. A short ride brought us to its head; and the sun now shining out, and the Prairie being clear before us, we pressed on as nearly west as we could, to find the river San Jacinto.

Two or three hours more brought us to that stream : but here we were once more at a loss, as we knew not whether Lynch's house was situated above or below us. While looking among the trees for some indication of our route, I heard the well known sound of a rattlesnake, and observed on the ground the largest and noblest reptile of the kind I had ever seen. I soon despatched him with a branch of a tree, and found that although he was five or six feet long, and about six inches in circumference he had but eight rattles; while one which I had killed a few days before of hardly half his size had thirteen, and several other small ones ten or eleven. I thought this afforded some evidence against the common opinion that the rattles denote the years of the animal's life. At length we discovered a path which had been recently travelled : but that afforded no information concerning the direction we ought to take. The San Jacinto is bordered there, as in other parts, by woodland; and its current is so gentle that I could not perceive that a stick I threw into the water moved either way. After some hesitation we again took the left hand route; but after a rapid ride of two miles, while the evening was coming on, we found a log hut, with an old woman, who told us that the house we were in search of was several miles up the river. Having five or six miles to go, although we spurred on impatiently, we were over-taken by the darkness, and encountered low and swampy land with other impediments, before we found our resting place. We had, however, ere this, got among droves of cattle, and passed a fence or two, by letting down the bars, so that we knew our journey was nearly at an end; and at length, after having travelled as we calculated, about sixty miles, we were hospitably received and comfortably fed and lodged.

On our arrival at Mr. Lynch's house, we found Mr. and Mrs. Burnet, whose acquaintance we had formed at Point Bolivar. He had recovered his steam boilers, which had been driven into the bay and to the land in so remarkable a man-ner, and was preparing to erect a house and a saw mill on the San Jacinto, near Mr. Lynch's, of whom he had purchased land just above, and with whom he and his workmen were temporarily accom-modated. I was convinced that he had acted wisely in taking a title of which there was no doubt, instead of getting one like my own, which he also intimated was not worth a farthing. On the advantages said to be offered in this vicinity for the operation of a saw mill, I have before remarked; and I now saw more of the abundance of fine cypress timber on the

banks of the San Jacinto, and the facility of floating it.

Cane brakes are common in some parts of Texas.
They are tracts of land low and often marshy, overgrown with the long reeds which we know in the
Northern States as fishing rods. They are sometimes found as underbrush in woods and forests, and
sometimes are not intermingled with trees, but form
one thick growth, impenetrable when the cane is dry
and hard. Our way led us the next day through one
of the latter description; and such a sight I never
before witnessed. The frequent passage of men
and horses keeps open a narrow path, not wide
enough for two mustangs to pass with convenience.
The reeds grow to the height of about twenty feet,
and are so slender, that having no support directly
over the path, they droop a little inward, and so meet
and intermingle their tops, forming a complete covering overhead. We rode thus about a quarter of a
mile, along a singular avenue, arched overhead, and
with the view of the sky shut out. The sight of a
large tract, covered with so rank a growth of an
annual plant, which rises to such a height, decays
and is renewed every twelvemonth, affords a striking
impression of the fertility of the soil.

Cane brakes often occur of great extent. Those
of a league, indeed of several leagues, are not uncommon. The largest is that which lines the banks of
Caney Creek, and is seventy miles in length, with

scarcely a tree to be seen in the whole distance. The reeds are eaten by cattle and horses in the winter, and afford a valuable and inexhaustible resource of food in that season when the Prairies yield little or none. At that time they are young and tender. When dry they are generally burnt, to clear the ground.

The next morning we set off for Harrisburgh. After riding for some time on the Prairie, we saw two animals which resembled black dogs jogging on before, to avoid us, and presuming they were wolves pursued them at full speed for some time. We found them much slower than we had expected, and gained on them so fast, that we must have come up with them in a short time, had they not reached a wood and so escaped us. Wild turkies repeatedly crossed our way a little before us, to which we several times gave chase for amusement, and found them more swift on foot than the wolves, as they could run about as fast as our horses. Deer too appeared and droves of horses, more numerous than before; and as the flowers seemed more abundant also, the ride was deficient neither in animal life nor in vegetable beauty.

Our way was no longer liable to doubt, as there was a path, sufficiently beaten to be discerned, on to Brazoria; and we proceeded to Harrisburgh over an irregular surface, no less gay with flowers and lively with wild animals than that we had already

16*

passed. At Harrisburgh the saw mill was working as lazily as before, although three vessels lay in the river, waiting for loads of lumber, for Mexican ports.

We found here the steamboat which was brought from New-York to Texas a few years since, by Capt. Henry Austin, laid up to rot in the San Jacinto. She was designed for use on some of the rivers of this country, and would doubtless have been serviceable to the inhabitants, as well as profitable to its owners, had the country been better settled. As yet however the people are too few, and the state of things such, that they are unprepared to give full employment to such a vessel. Mr. Austin, who brought the steamboat hither, is one of the remarkable members of a remarkable family. He has shown great enterprise and spirit of research, in some of his voyages to Asia, particularly in that during which he travelled up the Euphrates, and visited the site of Babylon. The interesting facts he stated on his return, have been substantiated by more recent travellers.

From Harrisburgh we passed in two days, over our former route, to Brazoria.

CHAPTER XXI.

WE found Brazoria already considerably improved, even in the short time since we had left it. Two or three houses had been completed, the first well was digging, and the aspect of the place showed that labor and pains had been bestowed in clearing away impediments and rubbish. As for my little horse, he also had returned in better case, so that tricks and travelling seemed to agree with him remarkably well. He was sent out to feed again from Mr. Austin's, to whom I was indebted for all the pleasure of his acquaintance, and with whom I now again took up my temporary abode. Here I was happy to have access to my baggage, which I had left behind, with the exception of a few necessaries; and a traveller in such a country as this sometimes realizes the comforts of a good wardrobe. I enjoyed a return to the place and people, with numbers of whom I felt well acquainted; and was ready to go back to the United States the first opportunity, without staying to visit any other part of the country.

Having satisfied myself that my money vested in a worthless land title had been wasted, and that the time I had spent had purchased only the gratification of seeing, I felt anxious only to return as speedily as possible. No vessel however was in Texas which could take me, and nothing remained but for me to await the arrival of one, of which we had hopes every day.

A considerable trade is carried on between this part of the territory and the interior of Texas, as well as the adjacent and even more distant Mexican States. I saw one day a row of fifty or sixty mules, just come in from the north. They were loaded with different articles to such a degree that I was astonished at their being able to travel, and compassionated them when I found how much they were worn out by their labors. They were, as usual, without bridle or halter, yet proceeded with perfect regularity in a single line, except now and then a couple of vicious ones were tied together side by side, whose tricks appeared to neutralize each other. The owners of the caravan, with several hired Mexican attendants, rode their mustangs, with their enormous spurs, weighing I suppose at least half a pound a piece, with rowels an inch and a half in length, and lever bits of the harshest description, able to break the jaws of their animals under a very gentle pressure. Overseen and directed by such an escort, and bowing under the burthen of three hun-

dred and sixty pounds without including the pan-
niers, which were bound on so tight as almost to
stop their breath, the poor mules formed a sorrowful
line; and came up spontaneously in turn to have
their girths unbound, and their loads removed.
They seemed scarcely able to keep upon their feet,
and as they successively obtained relief, one after
another heaved a long and deep sigh, which it was
painful to hear, because it proved that the poor
brutes had been worked beyond their strength.

The drivers of this caravan were anxious to sell
their horses, which they offered for six and eight
dollars a piece, having probably caught most of them
in the Prairies, or purchased them at trifling prices
of persons who had not been over particular in
obtaining them, as they bore a variety of marks.
Their value would have been considered very small
to a person returning through the region which they
had come from, certainly unless their brands had
been changed: for the owner of a horse may seize
him under any circumstances, if he finds his mark
upon him, unless it can be proved that he has sold
him. Mules being more useful in caravans, the
owner was not disposed to part with them. He had
been absent five or six months, passing through
Bexar I know not how far into the interior.

From the conversations which I held on the subject of this interior trade, I gathered, that the business
is attended with a variety of hazards and dangers.

Our countrymen do not readily bring themselves to look upon inland custom houses as the most rational institutions in the world; and, to men regularly engaged in smuggling, it is not surprising that the imposts laid by them on goods passing into particular towns should not seem the most righteous. At any rate these Texas traders complain of the duties they are often expected to pay; of the necessity of feeing Mexican officers in order to avoid them; and especially of the inconveniences, expense and imprisonment to which they are not unfrequently subject when they attempt unsuccessfully to set all at defiance. The trade is often very lucrative. Dry goods from the United States and a variety of light articles are carried into the interior of the Mexican Republic by this route, and sometimes find their way to the capital: for being admitted without duty into the ports of Texas, to favor the growth of the territory, while subject to considerable and sometimes heavy duties in the lower ports, they are in great demand in the country at good paying prices, that is, at two or three times the cost and charges. Tobacco forms an article of considerable importance in this trade: tobacco, which is contraband in the countries peopled from Spain as in Spain itself, and here as there long the cause of smuggling and crime. Heavy charges lie against this weed: it is here chargeable with breaking the rules of morality, as among us with violating those of good manners.

But there are other evils than those above mentioned, to which the overland trader in this country is liable. The caravans are often exposed to the attacks of Indians, who sometimes rob and even kill the owners. They therefore always go armed; and the conductor of one of these expeditions accompanied by his servants makes a formidable appearance. A great part of the attendants being Mexicans, however, they are probably more threatening than effective, at least if the common opinion of our countrymen who live among them is to be regarded: for they hold them in great contempt. The Indians also are generally supposed to be quite inferior to the colonists in the field, though more valiant and powerful than the others. The common saying is, that five Indians will chase twenty Mexicans, but five Americans (that is from the United States of the North,) will chase twenty Indians. Whether this is true or any part of it I cannot decide on personal knowledge: but certainly the Mexicans, although not very inferior in size, appear like a timid and inefficient race; and Indians are generally shot down without hesitation, whenever they present a fair mark, by any colonist who feels that acrimony against them which is apt to arise out of a sense of exposure to their attacks or ambushes. When they wander singly or in small parties far into the settlements, however, or when they are known to belong to certain tribes, they are not usually treated with unfriendliness, for then they are not expected to do injury. Some of them trade harmoniously at the towns, and even, as I have before mentioned, occasionally with the sea ports.

The common wages given to Mexican servants, are four dollars a month: but out of this contract abuses of a shameful nature too often arise. While a servant is in debt to his employer, the customs of the country allow the treatment of the former as a slave. He must continue the servant of that master until the debt is cancelled. Now the Mexicans being an ignorant, and apparently a harmless sort of people, sometimes incautiously receive supplies of cloths and other articles from their employers without counting the amount; and as the latter usually charge exorbitant prices—for instance a dollar a yard for common muslin—the poor fellow is in danger of being in debt a considerable sum over and above his wages. After this it is frequently easy to postpone for a long time his discharge. Traces of such abuses are to be found among some of the colonists in Texas; but I was informed that they prevail to a great extent in the interior, where some of the wealthy Mexicans have fifty or an hundred of their poor countrymen thus subject to them by a very unrighteous exercise of power. Things sometimes proceed so far, that when one absconds, he is advertised like a runaway slave.

One of the inhabitants of Brazoria with whom

I became acquainted on my former visit, I found making preparations for a trading journey into the interior, such as I have described. He took up his residence here on account of his health, which was bad in the United States, but has always been remarkably good in Texas. He had engaged the services of one of our enterprising countrymen, to aid in conducting his expedition to Bexar, and far beyond into the republic, and gave me a pressing invitation to accompany him, which I felt some disposition to accept. He was preparing packages of goods for the backs of mules, and calculating, with some reason, on returning in a few months with furs, specie, perhaps a few horses, &c. Specie is an important article in the return trade: but to see a few thousand dollars in silver wearing down the flesh of several good mules, is a lesson on the advantages of bank notes, or good bills of exchange, which enable us to send almost any amount we can get on a sheet of paper, and for single postage, all over the world.

I was now desirous of returning to the United States, and had hoped that on reaching Brazoria, I might hear of some vessel soon to sail for some of our ports. But in this I had been disappointed. I therefore determined to visit San Felipe, the seat of government and principal town of Austin's colony: indeed the largest town in all Texas. I had not felt particularly interested in such an excursion

17

before, because in so new a country very little is to
be looked for in the settlements, small and rude as
they must necessarily be.   The country itself, with
the condition and success of the colonists naturally
attract our chief attention, and to these I had paid
such regard as circumstances allowed.

A stranger looking over a map of Texas, particularly one of the later sort, might form erroneous
opinions of the state of the country, from the number
of places distinguished by names, like towns, the
designation of mere routes by lines, as if they were
well made and beaten roads.   The former, with few
exceptions, are in fact only large settlements in
anticipation, being now the sites of one or two
houses ; while the latter are often mere trackless
courses, such as I have described, laid through Prairies by the compass.   It is true, a great part of this
country, (with the exception of the mountain ranges
in the interior,) is so well fitted by nature for the
passage of travellers, and even for wagons, that little
need ever be done by art except in ferrying and
bridging streams ; yet when a tract of country is
marked with lines of roads, merely because it is in
a condition to be travelled on horseback, a person is
liable to form erroneous conclusions on other subjects,
necessarily connected with the existence of artificial
roads.   I was not surprised, with my knowledge of
the country, when after hearing that the route from
Brazoria to San Felipe was more travelled than any

other in the colony, I found that it was in many places indicated only by marked trees. I had often been on routes which maps represent as being well trodden, where I had not found this or any other intimation to guide my way.

CHAPTER XXII.

I was happy to find that two of my friends were
going to San Felipe : for I found I must spend some
time longer in the country, and had determined to
improve a part of the time in making a journey
thither. There was the residence of Colonel Stephen
Austin, the founder of the colonies of our countrymen in this delightful region ; and on the road and
in that vicinity were some of the oldest of the
settlements.

We left Brazoria in the afternoon of a pleasant
day, forming a party of four. Our road lay through
a forest, as we kept that day along the right, or
western bank of the Brazos, and on the bottom land,
as it is called. One of our number rode a fine,
large mule, which showed a very unmanageable and
vicious disposition, and often endeavored to rub his
master's legs against the trees. It was amusing to
see him pick out the largest, steer for them, and
exert himself to get against them. This was peculiarly inconvenient, as the rider had a negro boy

behind him, whom he was taking with him to sell.
We spent the night at Mr. Bell's house, on the
Brazos, where he found a purchaser. There was
only a house at the spot, though it is called Marion
on the maps.

The route from Brazoria to San Felipe usually
occupies nearly three days, especially when the roads
are in the bad condition in which we found them;
for though the distance is not very great, a horse
travels rather slowly, encumbered with considerable
baggage, and the traveller being liable to several
causes of delay, one of which we encountered.
The second day we left Bell's at an early hour,
under the direction of Mr. Westall, whose experience
in the country enabled him to guide us with advantage. The flies are very troublesome at this season
in this region; and when the heat came on we found
them intolerable. We had seen them before, and
observed the effects of their bite on our horses, but
never in such numbers as they now presented. A
hundred or more would fasten on each of our animals
at once, make a considerable wound in a moment,
and suck the blood abundantly, while the poor
creatures would show marks of extreme pain, and
shrink with dread whenever they felt their tormentors
light upon them. It was of little use to drive them
off, for they returned immediately and repeated the
bite in another place; and so deep was it, that every
spot they had touched was marked with a drop of

17*

blood. My poor little mustang being white, made the most pitiable appearance, being spotted with his own gore, so that he looked almost like a strawberry roan.

We now determined to retreat from the persecuting enemy, and entered the woods, where Mr. Westall assured us we should not be molested ; and found to our satisfaction that they did not leave the open ground. This is a fact well known to travellers in this country ; and it is common to lie by in the forest during the heat of the day. We found the shade agreeable, and refreshed ourselves abundantly with repose, even much longer than we desired : for it was not considered proper to proceed until the sun had got rather low, so that we waited there five or six hours. In walking about we found several places where hunters had been some months before, as we saw where they had made their fires, and trimmed the deer they had killed. It proved that they were Indians, who about two years before had come down as far as this region after game.

There are several tribes of Indians within the bounds of Texas. The Comanches in the N. West are rather numerous and very savage.

After leaving the woods we saw very few flies, and were surprised that the coolness of approaching evening had produced so sudden and perceptible an effect. The wind alone, I afterwards found, will prevent them from troubling the traveller even in hot weather. We proceeded on some miles farther along the Prairie, and saw many deer, and a few herds of wild horses. Having now learnt their habit of running in circles or semicircles when startled by passengers, we sometimes set off in different directions to meet them in their perambulations. On one occasion I took a course further to the left than any of my companions, and happened to meet a drove of about a dozen so nearly, that I might have shot one, if I had had a pistol in my hand. Though evidently shy, they did not turn or sheer off from their regular circuit. Much to my surprise I found at their head a fine, large, brindled mule, which must have strayed from some plantation, probably years before, and was now apparently quite wild. The herd followed him wherever he went; and this alone is sufficient to prove that the speed of the mustang is much inferior to that of the common horse, as the mule is comparatively slow. I spoke of shooting horses, for it is not uncommon in this country to put a rifle ball through them when other means of capturing them on the Prairies are not at hand. The people are so dexterous that they can generally shoot through the flesh just on the edge of the shoulder without causing a bad wound or much pain, yet so that the animal will instantly drop as if dead, probably shocked for a moment, and considering himself badly hurt. I have heard of the same practice being sometimes resorted to in the

Southern States, to stop runaway horses, but have never seen it.

The route we were on, between Brazoria and San Felipe, is the most travelled in Texas, and is pretty well settled, with houses kept as regular inns. There is of course less danger of hurting the feelings of any body by offering to pay for food and lodging. The uncertainty we had often been in, on leaving our stopping places, whether to pay or not, we had found embarrassing; and we had resorted to different devices to ascertain the humor of our hosts. Sometimes we would put a piece of money into the hands of a child, to see how the parent regarded it; and if we found it not likely to be well received, we could easily reclaim it. Now we regularly called for our bills on departing, as we freely asked for such things as we needed during our stay.

There is a remarkable elevation rising from the level surface of the Prairie, which we saw on this second day of our journey from Brazoria, which is famous through that part of the country. We first distinguished it from the distance of twenty miles, when though it appeared like a mere swell of no great height, was plainly perceptible from its contrast to the dead and uniform level around it. On it was situated a house at which we were to refresh; but but we had a long time to spend before we reached it. At length we reached the place, but although it occupied, as I mentioned, the summit of the knoll, it was very difficult to perceive any ascent to it, so gradual and so insignificant was the swell of that singular elevation.

As the heat came on, the flies began to trouble our horses, and at length we were compelled again to leave the road and betake ourselves to a shelter. We spent several hours, as on the previous day, partly in an old barn and partly in a shady wood, where we enjoyed an exemption from the vexatious insects which at that time infested the open ground. A person unacquainted with these terrible insects, would not easily be brought to credit the fact, though well established and unquestionable, that they some-times destroy the lives of cattle and horses, by the pain they inflict and the blood they draw from their veins.

It was near night before we found it prudent to pursue our journey, and then we moved on, as before, over a perfectly level and uniform surface, entirely destitute of rocks and stones, as it had been ever since we had left Brazoria.

I might have mentioned, while speaking of the inns on this route, that we found them always well supplied with various and excellent food, and of such descriptions as might be looked for in such a country. We had plenty of fresh bread, venison, wild turkey, beef, fowls, eggs, milk and good coffee; and usually slept well on comfortable beds. The custom-ary price for supper, lodging and breakfast was one dollar, including the feed of our horses: though we chose to take care of them ourselves. At some of these houses, as in many of those in Texas generally, we found one or more negroes, held as slaves, although the laws of Mexico forbid it. The blacks are ignorant, the whites are generally in favor of slavery and ready to sustain the master in his usurped authority: the province is so distant from the capital, and had been for some time so little attended to by the government, that the laws on this subject were ineffectual.

Negroes are even publicly sold; and about this time a colonist who had a large number, being alarmed at the report that a law had been passed in Mexico, providing for the collection of debts due abroad by residents in the republic, advertised and sold them at auction, though it was considered as rather a cover to his property, as most of them were purchased by one of his family connexions. I have before mentioned the device by which one of my fellow passengers from New Orleans evaded the Mexican law of emancipation: viz. by getting his negroes to sign a bond promising to serve him for ninety nine years. This man advised others to pursue the same course, and aided them in drawing up their papers. He afterwards sold a number of his own negroes to different purchasers.

The more we considered the nature of the "knoll" which I have before mentioned, the more singular did

it appear, that it should form so conspicuous an object
from so great a distance, and that it should be visible,
as we were informed it is, thirty miles off from the
northward. This was only a new evidence of the
extreme flatness of the great plains of Texas: for
such phenomena are not unprecedented. One in
Venezuela is mentioned by Humboldt, which although but a few feet high, is seen for many leagues.

The scene at the inn where we slept was enlivened
during the evening by the arrival of the hostess's son,
an enterprising man, with his caravan of loaded
mules, and four or five Mexican attendants, mounted
like himself on mustangs, armed and equipped after
the heavy and antiquated fashion of the country.
He expressed much satisfaction at his success in the
expedition, though the horses, of which he had
brought back a number bearing different marks, he
was anxious to sell at six and eight dollars apiece.

On the third day of our journey we passed several
houses, as we had done before. The colonists live
much as those whose estates I have heretofore described, and their estates usually bear a general
resemblance to them. Great quantities of cattle are
raised on the Prairies and bottoms, but there were
changes perceptible in some of the products of the
soil.

We were forced by the flies to waste several hours
in rest on the third day also, so that it grew dark
before we could see any thing of San Felipe. Soon

afterwards, however, the lights of that town made their appearance before us, though it was still, as we afterwards learnt, at a great distance. It is surprising that they should have been visible so far off: for we rode several hours directly towards them, and keeping them constantly in view, before we reached the place. The Prairie being uninterrupted by even the slightest variation of the surface, and clear of shrubs as well as trees, no obstacle was interposed; and, as we had no means for judging of the distance, we were deceived in a mortifying manner concerning the length of way which still lay before us. Of all tiresome rides I ever took this proved decidedly the most so; and as we pressed anxiously on, and the glimmering lights seemed to retire before us, we might almost have thought we were destined never to reach them.

CHAPTER XXIII

At length we arrived at San Felipe; and learnt
that one reason why we had seen the lights so far,
was the elevation of the ground on which the town
is situated. We found there were two public houses
in the place, and stopped at Whitehouse's, where we
lodged. In the morning we had an opportunity to
look around us.

San Felipe de Austin, (St. Philip,) stands on the
west bank of the Brazos, at the head of boat navigation, and on ground about 40 feet above the
surface of the water when at its usual level. From
the nature of the country where the river rises, and
the height of the banks, the floods rise here at particular seasons thirty feet. The shores are broken
sand banks, quite steep, and destitute of soil and
trees on the immediate margin of the stream, as
well as greatly deficient in beauty. The village, as
was naturally to be expected, presented nothing fine
or particularly interesting. It contains about fifty
houses, all built of logs, except one, which is framed,
and very comfortable. About a mile distant is the

residence of Mr. Williams, the secretary of Col.
Austin, from whom are obtained the land titles
conveyed to settlers.   Several wagons and other
carriages which I observed in the street gave an air
of business and thrift which I had not before seen in
Texas.

At the inn I found twenty or thirty men who had
come from different quarters in pursuit of places to
settle.   These persons, commonly called land-hun-
ters, were almost all from the United States, and
generally from the South Western States.   I saw
one, however, who had come from Ohio, and was
inquiring for a tract on which he might undertake
with advantage the raising of sheep.   Among these
strangers I found a number of very intelligent men :
but I learnt that a portion of them had fled from
justice, or as they chose to call it, from law, in their
own country.   It is a well known fact, that a considerable proportion of our countrymen who are found
in Texas, are of this character.   I saw at the breakfast table one morning, among those who were seated
with me, four murderers who had sought safety 'in
this country ; and a gentleman assured me, that on
one occasion, he had set down with eleven.

Men of this description often made the cause of
their emigration the subject of conversation, and
always spoke of themselves as having been unfortunately placed in circumstances in which it was
necessary to violate the laws, while they admitted no

criminality in their conduct. Duelists, of whom I
have seen a considerable number, always represented
themselves as having been so situated, that they
were compelled to shoot an antagonist to save their
own lives. Desha, the son of a governor of Tennessee, who fled for murder, died a little before my
arrival, confessing his crimes. So accustomed are
the inhabitants to the appearance of fugitives from
justice, that they are particularly careful to make
inquiries of the characters of new-comers, and gen
erally obtain early and circumstantial information
concerning strangers. Indeed it is very common to
hear the inquiry made : " what did he do that made
him leave home?" or "what have you come to Texas
for ?" intimating almost an assurance of one's being
a criminal. Notwithstanding this state of things,
however, the good of the public and of each individual
is so evidently dependant on the public morals, that
all appear ready to discountenance and punish crimes.
Even men who have been expatriated by fear of
justice, are here among the last who would be disposed to shield a culprit, guilty of a crime against life
or property. I can say more ; for, if I may judge
from evidences of general honesty and confidence
between man and man, I should think money would
be as safe without lock and key as in our own country. I am confident that if stores were left in some
parts of the United States without a watch and ex-

posed as many are in Texas, they would be robbed one of the first nights. The province having been until recently left without any regular courts, and being still very imperfectly provided for in this way, the inhabitants have thought it necessary in many cases to take the administration of punishments for public crimes into their own hands. Their inflictions, if not always the most just or judicious, are very apt to prove efficacious. In Brazoria, about the time of my visit there, a man strongly suspected of robbing a store, (and probably guilty,) was taken, whipped and cropped without judge or jury, and turned off to find his way out of the country as he could, but without any resort for satisfaction if he had been innocent.

In civil causes a process not less simple, but far more amicable and humane, was for a time pursued, especially in the infancy of the colony. I heard it spoken of as a thing within the knowledge of every body long enough a resident of the country to remember it, that when differences arose between men about property, the custom was to refer it to Colonel Austin, who merited and enjoyed the entire confidence of the inhabitants. In cases of peculiar stubbornness, or passion on one side, such as often hurry men into violent, protracted and expensive law suits, he repeatedly effected a reconciliation and arrangement by sitting for an hour on a log with the excited party, and conversing in such a manner as to allay his passions, and convince his judgment.

There is now at San Felipe an ayuntamiento, or council, an alcalde, or chief civil officer, and several persons of some education who perform the part of advocates, much on the principles of the laws of the United States. Men accused of high crimes are however made over to the Mexican authorities, at the seat of government of the state of Coahuila and Texas. Two men were now at San Felipe under a charge of murder, under keeping and restraint, but were allowed to move about the village.

A few native Mexicans are settled in this part of the province, and I witnessed one afternoon a Spanish fandango danced in the open air by a party of these people, evidently of a low class. There was nothing worthy of particular remark in the style of the performance; and the music, which was that of a violin, was poor indeed. A billiard table is publicly kept in the place, and found players even among such a limited population.

The situation of San Felipe struck me as agreeable, as the country near it is a little varied in its form. My impressions were however doubtless increased by the fact that I had long been familiar with the unvaried and tiresome level of the Prairies. The land was also variegated with visible divisions,

17*

in the village, to mark the bounds of private property. Keel boats occasionally pass to Brazoria, for the conveyance of freight: but the inconvenience of this navigation is so great, that the land route is generally preferred, though that is laborious and expensive in the present state of the country. The banks of the river are formed of soft loam, which renders poling boats very difficult; and in seasons when the waters rise, the current is very deep and rapid. It is probable that small steamboats will hereafter be introduced with great advantage on the Brazos. The water of this stream is always turbid, and particularly so when the floods are high.

There were several small stores in San Felipe, their stocks of goods being brought from New Orleans through Brazoria, chiefly by land, as before remarked. Most of the inhabitants of the town have lands in the vicinity: the terms offered by the Mexican Government through the empresarios, here as well as elsewhere in the province, being extremely tempting, to those who can submit to the laws of the country. Here were many persons who had come into possession, with good titles, of beautiful estates, merely for occupying them, and paying the expenses of surveying, recording &c., altogether not exceeding one hundred and fifty dollars. Single men are thus found, in the enjoyment of their quarter leagues: more beautiful and fertile, as well as more extensive than some old family possessions of

Europe, which have been objects of envy from age to age; and by merely becoming a married man, each is entitled to an addition of three times as much more, instead of becoming by that measure, as in many other parts of the world, almost of necessity a beggar.

CHAPTER XXIV.

THE settlement of San Felipe was commenced in 1824 by Colonel Austin. His father, Moses Austin, who, as it would appear, first formed the project of introducing settlers from the United States into Texas, was a native of Durham, Connecticut. Mrs. Holley mentions, in her "Letters on Texas," that he first proposed to attempt something on this subject in 1819: and in 1821 was authorised by the Spanish authorities in Mexico to introduce three hundred families into Texas. In consequence of fatigues and exposures incurred during his journey through the wilderness from Bexar to the United States, however, he soon after died, leaving an injunction on his son, Colonel Stephen F. Austin, to prosecute his plans. He commenced a settlement on the Brazos river in December, 1821; but the colony suffered extreme want from the loss of the two cargoes of provisions sent out for them from New Orleans. One was lost on the coast, and the other was taken after landing by the Indians. They lived for some time on the mustangs they killed on the Prairies, and are said to have eaten about one hundred of them. Indians, belonging to several tribes, at that time occupied the country around them, and constantly exposed them to danger. In 1824 Col. Austin was required to make a journey by land to Mexico, to get the approbation of the republican government to the progress of his colony ; and in the existing state of the country ran many risks, during a journey of twelve hundred miles. Having succeeded, he returned: but found that many of the settlers had gone back, and that others who had come out to join him, had established themselves at Nacogdoches and the Trinity river. Since that time the colony has been increasing ; and its success has gradually made known to the citizens of the United States something of the advantages of the soil and climate, and attracted many settlers, particularly from Tennessee, Alabama, Kentucky, and other southern and western states. It is strange, however, that the peculiar terms on which settlements are invited and allowed by the Mexican laws should have been unknown to so great an extent among us, and that so much should have been overlooked and so much presumed upon without inquiry or proper investigation.

Colonel Austin, in obtaining the authority to procure settlers for his grant or colony as it is called, acquired no right to the soil, but only the powers of an agent for the government, to give titles to settlers on condition of occupancy, and the right of having five leagues for every hundred settled under his direction, without expense to the government. His position, however, has secured other advantages to himself, and he has now as I understood, become proprietor of many valuable tracts of land in different parts of the province: first, by locating his five league tracts, and secondly, in the following manner. There have been not a few settlers who found it impossible to pay even the hundred and fifty dollars charged as expenses on each grant to a settler; and in advancing it for them, he has often taken a lease of the land for ninety-nine years. I was informed that he had now about seventy leagues, for some of which he had refused three dollars an acre. These leagues, it will be remembered are Mexican, and equal to forty-four hundred and twenty acres and a fraction, English.

The principal objection to becoming a colonist in this country, arises out of the intolerance of the laws. Protestants are not allowed to have places for public worship, and the legitimacy of no marriage ceremony is acknowledged unless performed by a Roman Catholic priest. Under the government then existing, viz: that commonly called the usurpation of Busta- mente, there were no hopes of any improvement in this respect, as the interests of the nation were oppo- sed to those of the rulers, whose chief supporters were the Europeans and the clerical and aristocratical natives. It is however generally believed by experienced and intelligent men in our own country, that the Roman Catholic system is by nature inimical to republicanism, and that both cannot have at once the ascendency. Some of the most patriotic and experienced among the Mexican and South American statesmen are also known to have adopted the same opinion, after having seen a long and disastrous contest between these two systems. The clerical as well as the papal power has been impaired in Mexico; and if they are ever so far overcome as to permit the establishment of religious toleration, the principal objection against forming settlements in Texas will be removed. Until that time arrives, this objection will appear to many persons decisive.

One day during my stay at San Felipe, I witnessed a ceremony which would have been regarded as a very extraordinary thing in our own country. A Roman Catholic priest had arrived there, on a tour of visitation through the colony, and offered to perform baptismal and marriage ceremonies for all who might wish to receive them. Having been invited where he was to receive applications and administer, at a particular house in the village, I attended with two or three friends, to see what would be done. Several settlers from the United States, who I knew had no inclination in favor of Roman Catholicism, and though they had received a Protestant education, presented themselves for baptism. These, as I had reason to believe, acted merely on a wish to recommend themselves to the favor of the government. Several afterwards came with their wives, and were married again, lest the legality of the Protestant ceremony should not be acknowledged, and stand as a bar between their descendants and their estates.

The priest stated that he had married about five and twenty in one evening in some place in the country, where many colonists had assembled on timely notice being given of his visit. He was a jolly looking old man, with very little of that sedate, venerable or even intelligent aspect which we associate with an aged minister in our country. He showed some inclination to jest on the occasion. One of the young men who was standing ready for baptism caught my eye, and smiled. "You must not laugh," said the old man, "if you do you will always afterwards be laughing christians: if you are sober now you will be sober christians all your lives."

One day my attention was attracted in San Felipe by above fifty mules, composing a caravan which had just arrived from somewhere to the northwest. They were under the charge of eight or ten men, who were principally Mexicans, and some of them tall and large. The ponderous saddles and packs seemed to me heavy enough alone to load the poor beasts; but beside these they had to carry three hundred and sixty pounds weight. Many of them were loaded with specie; and all appeared, like the beasts in the other caravans I had seen, to be excessively fatigued.

There is something strange in the idea of a considerable branch of trade being carried on over regions of great extent destitute of roads and all indications to mark routes; yet such I understood was the nature of the country above this place. Among the persons I saw at the inns were men who had come from the United States by land, from Natchitoches through the unsettled tracts north-east of us. The road, which is often spoken of as an old one, and is laid down on many maps, is however a mere route, marked out by notched or blazed trees, (that is, trees with a broad piece of the bark cut smoothly off.)

19

CHAPTER XXV.

As there was yet no arrival of a vessel from the United States, and of course no prospect of a passage thither at least for a couple of weeks, I felt favorably disposed to make a journey a little further into the country, especially as it would probably prove much cheaper than to remain in the town, and two of my friends were about to set off on such an excursion. Before we took our departure, we met with a judge from Alabama, who was looking out for land to purchase, with the intention of making a settlement; and he determined to accompany us. In the region before us we had to look for nothing like inns, and must anticipate receiving only such accommodations as we could find at the scattering estates we might meet with, or, when none were to be found, taking up with what we could obtain in the uninhabited country.

Every body we had conversed with had described the land as excellent and the climate agreeable; and we had reason to concur in their judgment, from the first glimpses we caught on our journey. We had changed the smooth and apparently endless levels over which we had travelled so long, for a " rolling country," which presented us a constant and agreeable succession of hill and dale ; and as the woodland was more abundant, the eye was relieved with another sort of variety also, which is perhaps as necessary to its gratification, as an occasional irregularity of surface.

The undulating or rolling country is distinguished from the extensive levels below by several marked characteristics. Lying between them and the mountain range for seventy and an hundred miles, it is more elevated than the former, and perpetually varying the surface, but without breaking into ridges or rising to high hills. Beyond Red river the timber is confined to the borders of streams, and is not, as here, plentifully intermingled with open Prairie land. Not only is the scenery beautiful, but the country is more healthful, the soil dark, fertile and well watered. Insects are not troublesome here as below, except the flies, which still tormented our horses. Every thing which is cultivated on the level will flourish here, except long staple cotton and sugar cane. Rocks useful in building are also found, which are entirely wanting below, particularly lime stone. Mrs. Holley remarks that these regions are as favorable as the levels to cattle and hogs, and better for sheep and horses, while experiments have proved that wheat, rye, oats and flax may be cultivated with success.

After a ride of five or six miles we reached a creek where we found one of those rare but most useful establishments, a saw mill. Log houses may satisfy the first settlers in a country, especially if the means of subsistence are precarious and demand the whole attention of the colonists, or if there be dangerous enemies at hand to be apprehended. Such was the state of Texas until within a few years. But now, when there is abundance of food and nothing is apprehended from the savages, people begin to think of their convenience, and to ask for something better than logs to construct their dwellings of.

We stopped for some time at the saw mill, and conversed with the owner, who welcomed us into his house. He had a noble field of corn, and other signs of prosperity around him. At his table, (for we dined with him,) we found excellent fare, and that in abundance; but had been forewarned, and afterwards more fully realized, that we must put up with more simple food than we had generally been supplied with before. Flour we could not long expect to see, nor any thing composed of it: it is a luxury here, the transportation being so expensive, as to forbid its use to persons of the poorer class. The stream on which the mill was erected, we were informed, is raised by the floods thirty feet above its ordinary level. Near this place I saw the first wild rye I ever met with. It was growing in bunches here and there, and bore a general resemblance to common rye, but was considerably smaller. I often saw it afterwards. Here also for the first time I saw wild indigo, which is preferred to that of the Southern States.

As we proceeded beyond, we found the country presenting many beautiful scenes: the open natural fields, destitute of bushes of all sorts as well as of trees, were generally smooth and uniform in their appearance, though spread over an undulating surface, while the groves and woods which here and there interrupted it were disposed with a degree of beauty quite singular. We had now to expect inhabitants only at great intervals, the population being much more thin in this part of the colony: so that we could not find a habitation in less than ten, twenty, and in some cases thirty miles, and then not always even a comfortable one. We had already begun again to find frequent use for our compass, which, we had been informed, must be our principal dependance during our excursion. There is however a general direction which all travellers take in this part of the colony, as may be seen from the map. It lies along between the Brazos and Colorado rivers, nearly midway, and between the heads of their numerous branches. The brooks are generally bad to cross; and it is better to avoid them, even at the expense of a little circuitous travelling, than to attempt the fords, which a stranger cannot often find.

Keeping thus in the general direction of the two rivers by the aid of the compass: that is about North North West, we occasionally bent our course to the right or left to head some tributary of the two streams, or deviated this way or that as the varying surface of the undulated ground offered an easier passage. Sometimes also the beauty of a scene would attract us a little out of our direct course: for, the further we proceeded, the more were our surprise and pleasure excited by the increasing richness of the landscape. We had ever before us a smooth but swelling surface, with open lawns, patches and groves of wood, where narrow vallies wound between gentle acclivities, here and there overshadowed by thick trees, which in some places occupied the summits of the hills, and in others skirted their bases or spread down their sides. Having nothing to confine our course within any fixed limits, and feeling always that our course was an unsettled one, we were often in doubt whether to take the vale on this or that side of some little eminence before us, and were ready to stand and hesitate, being equally pleased with both the verdant routes that lay before us.

We spent the night at the house of a colonist evidently of the poorer class. Flour was there but little known; but we were furnished with cakes made of Indian meal, which were very good, though unaccompanied by the variety of meats which we had found at the inns of San Felipe and on the road thither. Here I tasted the first good water I had found in Texas: that in the lower country being inferior, and almost without exception obtained from brooks or rivers. Our host, however, in his poverty was rich in a good well, and in water of a much improved quality: for we were now in a soil more abundant in rocks, and of a different nature from that we had left.

We were somewhat amused by observing the rather rough and uncouth manners of two young men from a retired settlement, some distance inland, who stopped here on their way to San Felipe. They seemed to relish as highly as we did some of the plain but wholesome food which was placed before us; and one of them, after taking a large draught of some of the richest milk in the world, turning to his comrade, said with peculiar emphasis: "If we could take this milk along with us in our gourd, and have it fresh on the Prairie, I tell you, it would be nauceous."

CHAPTER XXVI.

HAVING nothing to hasten us on our journey faster than our convenience dictated, and being free from anxiety, as well as the apprehension of any difficulty, we often resorted to such devices as travelling sometimes suggests to beguile the way. One of our party, as we had observed, always disappeared on stopping at a house, running in to talk with the inhabitants, thus to ingratiate himself that he might obtain the best accommodations, leaving us to take care of our horses. On reaching our stopping place on the second evening, after we had as usual been left to put out our horses into the Prairie ; and while we were rubbing down our mustangs and hobbling them, a negro boy came out of the house under peremptory orders from our companion within, to see to his horse. One of our party, who possessed a good share of roguish ingenuity, after some inquiries about the gentleman in the house, how he looked, and what he was doing, told the boy in rather a low voice, that he had better not come nearer to him than was necessary, for it was possible he might hurt him, though still he did not think he would. The boy asked why he need be afraid of him. He replied that he did not certainly know that there was any reason—he hoped there was none—but the man had been bitten by a mad dog, and it was rather uncertain whether he was not growing mad himself. Still he would not alarm the boy, but cautioned him not to be afraid, for there might be no danger, though there was something rather strange in the conduct of his poor friend. This was enough for the boy: he was almost afraid to touch the horse of such a man; and when, a moment afterwards, our companion came out of the house, he slunk away behind the horse, and though he was in a great hurry to get him unsaddled, kept his eyes fixed steadily on the owner, closely watching his motions.

"Take off that bridle!" exclaimed the impatient traveller, in a stern voice; and the black boy sprung off and darted away as fast as his feet could carry him, much to the vexation and surprise of our companion, who ran after him a little distance, but could in no way account for his singular and provoking conduct. When we entered the house, things appeared a great deal more strange: for the negro had rushed hastily into the midst of the family, and in his terrified state communicated the alarming tale, that the gentleman had been bitten by a mad dog. He, unconscious all the time of what an effectual trick was playing off, endeavored as usual to render himself as agreeable as possible, by pleasant conversation with the inmates, and especially the females, with whom he had already formed a partial acquaintance. We could see that they looked on him with marked apprehension, and retreated whenever he approached them. One of them took an opportunity to inquire of the story-teller the truth of his own charge; and his answer confirmed their fears and redoubled their caution, though after confessing, with apparent candor, that his friend had been bitten, he stated that there was no certainty of evil consequences, and it was a thing which of course could not be mentioned to the sufferer. As bed time approached, the mistress of the house expressed her fears lest trouble should arise in the night; for the house, according to custom, contained but two rooms, and was not built for security. She therefore urged us to sleep between him and the door, and by no means to let him pass us. It so happened, however, that he chose to sleep next the door for the sake of the air; and it was with great difficulty that we could keep their fears within bounds. The ill disguised alarm of the whole family, was not less a source of merriment to him who had been the cause, than of surprise and wonder to the subject of it. Whatever member of the household he approached promptly withdrew; and as for the negro, whenever he was spoken to by him, he would jump and roll his eyes.

In the morning, when we were about to depart, we commissioned our belied companion to pay our bill : but as he approached the hostess, she fled from him, and shut the door in his face. " I want to pay our bill !" said he. " Oh, if you will only leave the house," cried she in terror, " you are welcome to your lodging."

On the third day two of my companions returned to San Felipe, so that I pursued the remainder of my journey in company only with my judicial friend from Alabama. Scenes similar to those already described were still presented to us; and no description which I can give, will do them justice. Surely no land could be found in any part of the world, where nature has done more to give the landscape the aspect of art. The smooth lawns spread their unvarying coat of green over the swelling surface, still bearing the name of Prairie, which is not confined to the levels as is sometimes erroneously supposed. On one side they would often wind up a narrow valley, while on the other they terminated suddenly at a clump or grove of noble forest trees, which rose stately and tall as if not only planted, but pruned by an experienced hand. The proportions between the open grounds and woodland, with their disposition and arrangement, continually impressed the mind with a vague idea that they were all the effects of human calculation and design; and although we often saw neither a habitation, nor discovered the footstep of a human being or a domestic animal, for more than twenty miles together, we never felt alone or seemed fully to realize that we were in a "desert wherein dwelleth no man." Here we occasionally saw repeated a natural phenomenon, of all others, perhaps the most nearly resembling a work of art : viz ; those long ranges of forest where the outer trees form a perfectly straight line, and spring from the grass of the Prairie without a bush or a sapling about their roots. The meeting of two such lines, I have also contemplated with surprise, where it seemed as if a fine field had been brought to one of its angles, and nothing was wanting but a fence to complete the resemblance to enclosed land. The open ground every where looked as if a cultivator would have only to put in his ploughshare, drop his seed, and await his harvest ; and from many points a passenger could fancy he might select in the imaginary estates of wealthy proprietors, the arable land and pasturage, and the spot designed for the orchard ; while patches of brilliant flowers seemed to show a splendid garden already in bloom.

We now realized, what our friends had told us ; that the country was rich and delightful, but needed to be visited to be known. No words can do justice to its peculiar appearance, or excite the feelings which we experienced in travelling in it, especially when we wandered, as we often did, through unmeasured fields of flowers, with nothing but the compass to dictate our course, while every thing seemed equally attractive on every side.

Our enjoyment was doubtless enhanced by attendant circumstances. Having nothing to press us on faster than we pleased to go, we were at liberty to proceed at any gait, or to repose at any hour, provided only that we used the precautions necessary to bring us to a habitation before night. We had not the wearisome view of the level and uniform Prairie before us, and (with the exception of flies,) were relieved from the annoyance of troublesome insects, some of which, particularly the musquitoes, had often given us great vexation in the lower district, while the rolling country is happily free from them.

We found the wild rye very common in these regions, which is considered a sign of very good land wherever it is found. We saw also the wild plum : a short bush, which bears an esteemed fruit, of which on account of the season, we of course had no opportunity to judge. On the few cultivated estates we saw, cattle were reared as below. The corn was about as high as my shoulders, and rapidly growing, being the tall corn of the south. What subsequently struck me, was, that in passing at a moderate rate of travelling, not long afterwards, along the Mississippi and to the Middle and Eastern States, I found the season apparently growing a little more backward till I ended my travels in August, and no where in advance of what it was in this region of Texas, from the middle to the last of May.

The most common grain in this part of the country is Indian corn. On one estate I saw about an acre and a half of wheat, the only instance in which I saw it growing in this country. Last year, as the proprietor informed us, it produced a good crop; and when we saw the field, the grain was flourishing. This is sufficient to show that the common opinion may be well founded; viz: that this upper country is favorable to wheat. Until mills shall have been erected, however, wheat will never be extensively cultivated : for it would now be an unprofitable crop, although the price of flour is about twenty-five dollars a barrel: so expensive it is to transport it from the landing at Brazoria.

It was pleasing to find here a great plenty of running streams, abundantly sufficient to water the country. Rocks and stones also abounding in the soil, offer excellent materials for the construction of fences, as well as of better houses than those we had seen, while they presented a feature hitherto unknown to me in Texas.

of it lies a smaller tract of land, called Austin's New Colony, beyond which is another, called Williams and Austin's, where as yet few settlers had been introduced. The nature of the surface, the quality of the soil, the productions and climate, as I was informed, continue much the same for a great distance beyond, and must hereafter invite numerous settlers, when circumstances shall be more favorable.

The liberal and tolerant views of the government of Mexico at the time when the first part of this book was writing, were such as to encourage the hope that our countrymen might be admitted without being required to renounce Protestantism. In that case, if the country had continued to enjoy peace and prosperity, and land had still been given to foreign emigrants on the same terms, no doubt these extensive and attractive regions would have become rapidly occupied; being brought into powerful competition with the wild lands within our own borders, and particularly those in the adjacent states. But until some sure guarantee is given, there can be no sufficient security offered to Protestants, that they or their children will be allowed to worship God according to the dictates of their conciences. A revolution has recently occurred, which has given the priests and anti-reformers the ascendancy.

The following morning we set off on our return. Having got some information concerning the number, situation and bearings of the settlements near our

CHAPTER XXVII.

Travels north of San Felipe, (*continued.*)—North-west corner of Austin's Colony.—Wild horses, deer, buffalo.—Dread of Indians.—The Colorado river.—Returning.—Appearance of strangers on a Prairie.—Rencontre.—Lose our way.—San Felipe.

ONE of my companions had accompanied me further than the others, because he wished to inspect a tract of land he had obtained near the north-western corner of Austin's Colony. Beyond that angle we did not design to go; and on approaching the Colorado river near that point, we regarded it as the end of our excursion. The last colonist we found in that direction, was a man who had emigrated some years before from Pennsylvania; and had acquired a comfortable property in a short time through the luxuriance of the soil. He was surrounded, though at no inconsiderable distances, by settlers from different parts of the United States. We saw that we were in a wilder country, so far as related to game and wild animals, than any we had seen; for having gradually arrived among a thin population, and approached somewhat nearer the regions inhabited by Indians, we occasionally perceived the tracks of buffalo, which are not uncommon there, and heard

of wild hogs, bears and panthers.   One of the swine
we had seen dead at a house at which we had stopped
a few days before.   It had been shot, and though not
large, appeared like rather a formidable animal, being
armed with tusks of considerable length, which
curled back from his under jaw.   The animal was
greyish, and of a disagreeable aspect.   According to
common report they have sometimes attacked men.

Our host having proposed an excursion to the very
extremity of the colony, we accepted it, and, mounting our horses, accompanied him on a ride over a
very pleasant, though unoccupied region.   We were
still annoyed by flies.   We saw deer and mustangs
in herds, and frequently noticed the fresh marks of
buffalo, which are often killed hereabouts.   We had
left our guns at San Felipe, considering them almost
as useless as burdensome ; but we had our pistols
with us, and our new companion went better armed
with his rifle.   We soon perceived that he was under
constant apprehension of Indians, and that an unceremonious fashion which prevailed, of shooting
down red men wherever they were found, was the
order of the day.   He recounted tales of savage
murders perpetrated on settlers and travellers at
different times ; and would often interrupt himself
or us to say : "How I would shoot an Indian if he
should jump out of the bushes yonder!"   He would
look, and act too, as if he really expected to meet
every moment with such an unwelcome traveller.

We now began to think we had not do
in leaving our guns at San Felipe : for it s
if a settler, well acquainted with the cou
heretofore engaged in savage warfare,
entertain such apprehensions of an enem
there was some real danger.   We had bef
admitted a thought of fear from such a qua
now, the more we thought of the vast regi
of us, free to the passage of a wily and rap
thinness of the population around us, an
fenceless condition of the frontier, the more
to participate in the feelings of our hos
scrutinize the groves and thickets as we pas
with uncommon care.   However, we
nothing to alarm our fears any further ; a
were to turn our faces for San Felipe the
we congratulated ourselves that we should
reason for further apprehension.

The direction we had taken, (road there
brought us at length to the left bank of th
river, there a small stream at this seaso
sometimes, like the other Texas rivers, it i
a considerable height.   We turned and
down its course for some distance, and
leaving it, we returned to the house of our

We were now at the north-western corn
is commonly called Austin's first colon
as I have elsewhere remarked, this ter
understood here in a very limited sens

route, which was further to the east than that which we had travelled before; we intended to visit in succession those at which we might most conveniently dine and spend the three nights we had before us.

Though we had become familiar with the appearance of the country in this part of the province, we were nevertheless sometimes almost convinced again that the rich and beautiful region around us was inhabited by men like ourselves. No tokens of neglect were to be seen, no signs of that rudeness and roughness which we look for in a wilderness. It seemed as if nothing but the industrious hand of man could have removed fallen trunks and branches from the neat borders of the woods, or checked the growth of weeds and bushes which are so forward to rise and deform a lonely lawn. It was exceedingly difficult to believe, even after repeated experience, that the peace which reigned around us was the tranquillity of desertion, and that the general stillness was the silence of death. The universal quiet seemed ever ready to be interrupted by the distant low of cattle, the whetting of a scythe, or the bell of a village church: each of which would have been to my mind accordant with the scene, especially the last: for the calmness of all things seemed calculated to remind one of the Sabbath. With such impressions, amidst such scenes, we wound our way at leisure, following the general indications of

the compass, but constantly making slight deviations
from it, as the form of the ground, or the absence of
trees opened our way most invitingly on the left or
the right. The extent of Prairie land, or open
ground, still preponderated over that covered with
forest trees, so that our prospects were often very
extensive.

It was on such a tract we were riding in the course
of the day, when, looking at a distant part of the
Prairie on the east, we discovered what we thought
was a drove of mustangs approaching us. In a few
moments, however, we perceived human beings,
when our attention was much more strongly attracted, as our late fear, immediately suggested the idea of
Indians. After watching them for a few moments,
we ascertained that there were about a dozen men,
moving with considerable rapidity. We agreed that
it would be most prudent to avoid them if possible,
and turning our horses in an opposite direction, spurred them on at as quick a pace as their weariness
would permit. So many savages, thought we, with
only two men to deal with, and these armed only
with pistols—this would be a hopeless case if they
are such relentless beings as our host had described.
While endeavoring to make our escape, we put our
pistols in order, though with a sincere hope that we
should have no occasion to use them : but we soon
satisfied ourselves, on looking back, that we were
discovered by the strangers, and that an interview

would be unavoidable. We then concluded that we had nothing to do but to advance with all the appearance of confidence and friendliness we could assume : and turning our horses, we proceeded directly towards them.

We had now a better opportunity to scrutinize their appearance : much better indeed than we desired ; and it did not diminish our alarm to find that they had a wild look, were mounted, armed with long weapons, and rode without regularity at a headlong rate. We were now able to count them, and found there were ten of the party : but as we rapidly approached each other, we found they did not appear exactly like Indians, but though in rather rough and singular clothes, were not dressed at all like savages. Their complexions, when we were able to distinguish them, explained all this. They were white men ; and, as soon as we met, testified much joy at the rencontre, and showed great anxiety to obtain information about the country. They were Tennessee farmers, and had just arrived from the United States, by the way of Natchitoches, that is, the old route which the Spaniards used for two hundred years, and which is now annually travelled by the caravans from the Red river to Santa Fe. They were armed with long rifles, and one of them carried behind him the quarters of a deer they had killed and skinned.

These men, with a general knowledge of the fertility of the soil, the genial nature of the climate, and the terms on which the Mexican government grant titles, had sold their estates in Tennessee, and had come on to take up their residence in this province. Ignorant of the country itself, and destitute alike of guides and land marks, they were coursing about in high spirits, yet at a venture, after the general indications derived from their compass, and with their own experience in wild regions, towards the lower settlements. We gladly gave them all the information in our power on such subjects as they inquired about, and after a short but friendly interview, took leave and parted from them.

But we had not gone far before we began to doubt and to differ about our own course; and after much reflection and conversation, on the time we had occupied and the different courses we had steered, could agree but upon one thing and make but one discovery, and that was, that we were lost. This was rather a painful truth to be acknowledged, but it was indisputable. Our circumstances were even more unpleasant than when our party wandered on the Prairie west of the Trinidad : for then we had some determinate objects to seek : first Goose creek and then the San Jacinto. But now we had no landmark to look for, and were probably ten if not twenty miles distant from the nearest habitation. We wandered about over the open Prairie and sometimes through groves and woods, until we had serious apprehensions of having to spend the night in the open air, and, what was worse, of going without food: for we had no means to procure any.

After wandering thus for two or three hours, we were happy at discovering a house, at which we were hospitably received by an old woman, who had little but the barest necessaries to offer us. She soon set before us a meal of which we stood in need, and which was a welcome repast to us, although it consisted only of pork fried with onions, tops and all. Her simple house and table furniture were worse for wear, and one of our forks had but one prong. She seated herself with us, and immediately began a regular and prolonged lamentation over her fate as a Texas colonist. She said that although the country was healthful and productive, her husband not unprosperous and her children well, she regretted the time when she left the United States, a country where there were neighbors, for a distant land where there was nothing to see or hear.

After leaving this place, we travelled some distance further, when we saw cattle feeding on the Prairie, and knowing this to be the usual indication of neighboring inhabitants, soon found a house, where we made a short stop. The master and mistress, as we were informed, were on a visit to a neighbor some twenty or thirty miles distant. We were invited in, however, and learnt more of the character of the colonist than pleased us, from a hasty examination of a few books we picked up : Tom Paine and kindred writers—what miserable commentaries on the nature of their owner—what miserable associates for the solitude and leisure of these regions, especially to a man in the decline of life !

We stopped again at Bell's saw mill, and there met a man, who, we were informed, was preparing to make a settlement in the neighborhood, and occasionally preached at private houses. He was a methodist, but had encountered no obstacles in conducting religious worship in this manner. Of this, however, under existing circumstances he could have no security. The laws and prejudices are against it.

On the road from this place to Brazoria, our attention was attracted, as it had often been in other places on our route, to the extraordinary size of the grape vines, which are very numerous in the woods. It was no uncommon thing to find their stocks as large in circumference as a man's body. We found the black mulberry trees also very abundant. They were at this season covered with ripe fruit, on which we regaled ourselves, by only riding under the shade, and picking the mulberries sitting in our saddles.

I had been absent from San Felipe six days, and my expenses had amounted to just five shillings. The people I had been among had not permitted me to pay for food or lodging ; and the small sum I had got rid of I had distributed among such of their children as would receive a little money.

On reaching San Felipe again, I took up my lodgings once more at Whitehouse's. I found two old acquaintances in the town : the two Frenchmen we had delivered from the New Orleans schooner. These poor fellows, after losing their little cargo, which was not insured, and having been subject to considerable expense, were waiting for an opportunity to return to the United States.

Vegetables of various kinds and excellent quality we found now abundantly supplied from gardens in the vicinity, and we had beans, peas, potatoes and onions. The settlers generally pay but little attention to such articles, or at best content themselves with securing a supply for their families, though a little care would ensure them almost any supposable quantity, such is the favorable nature of the soil and climate. Cat fish are caught in the Brazos. Cattle of course are abundant and cheap. A cow was worth from eight to ten dollars. Persons come here every year to purchase cattle to drive to the Red river for New Orleans.

During a walk I took by the river, I saw an Indian and his squaw preparing to cross the stream, by beginning to take off their clothes. Seeing me they modestly retreated, and when I next saw them they had betaken themselves to the water. In order to convey their garments across without wetting, they had resorted to an expedient, which, simple as it is, I never had before seen adopted, but which I must mention.   They placed them upon a short log which they had picked up; and this while it saved them the trouble of tying them upon their heads as I should have done, afforded them aid in swimming, as each rested one hand upon it.

CHAPTER XXVIII.

THIS Indian I had observed in the town, and admired him as the handsomest man I had ever seen. He was tall, strait, well proportioned, and moved with native ease and dignity, bearing a general resemblance to our northern Indians, though much surpassing any of them I had ever met in personal beauty. His dress was little more than the waist cloth and blanket; and in this he resembled several others I had seen, who had come from the interior to sell their deer skins. The woman was dressed with more care and taste.

I returned to Brazoria by the way I had before travelled, in company with six or seven agreeable companions; but found it much impeded in several places by the swelling of the streams. Some of these, through which we had then easily waded, were now so deep that our horses were obliged to swim them. As usual, we had our jests to play upon each other, which served to turn the laugh of the party on one and another by turns. One of our jokes I had afterwards serious reason to remember. One morning some of our number had been particularly facetious, and I was rather a sufferer by one of their practical jests : for while we made a stop at noon to refresh ourselves at one of the houses on the way, my large, broad-brimmed hat was unaccountably withdrawn, and when my companions remounted it was no where to be found. Without being altogether pleased at having such a liberty taken with me, I affected more discontent than I actually felt; and tying my handkerchief upon my head, I sprung upon my white mustang, and rode on with more gravity than usual, though I presumed that some one privy to the trick would take care that it should not be left behind.

I rode on however about four miles, suffering considerably from the heat of the sun, against which I had always been well protected, and yet nothing had been seen of my hat. I had, on the contrary, been bantered by some of my friends with a story of its lying in pawn at the house we had left. The traveller who had deprived me of it now finding that I was resolved not to return for it, began to repent his jest, and offered to go back and bring it to me, on condition that the past should be forgotten, and there should be no more retaliation. I consented to the terms; so, lighting a segar with his sun glass, and mounting his mule, he set off at a rapid rate on his return. He had not been gone long, when one of the party presented me with my hat, which he had secretly brought along with him. It was long before our absent horseman overtook us, having spent some time in useless inquiries; and when he perceived the object of his ride upon my head, and recollected the promise by which he had thoughtlessly bound himself, while he had bound me, not to have any more jesting, he could only exclaim—"Well, it's hard, but it's fair."

At night I felt an unusual sensation of fatigue, and slept hard without being much refreshed; while on the following day I found myself rather languid and depressed.

I felt somewhat indisposed for several days at Brazoria, but well enough to attempt a short excursion, and repeated my visit to Mr. McNeil's and Mr. Westall's. I found every thing flourishing, and the rural scene wearing the aspect of greater luxuriance than when I saw it before. While at the latter place I was seized with the fever and ague with violence, so that I was unable to leave the house, and was compelled to accept the kind and urgent offer of Mr. Westall and his family to remain with them. They paid every attention, and rendered me as comfortable as circumstances would permit: but I suffered severely.

There was a school kept in the house at that time by Mr. Phelps, who had been in Captain Partridge's Academy in the Northern States. It was

attended by the children of the family, by those from
Mr. McNeil's and another neighboring estate, who
come daily, although the distance was considerable;
and by two or three others from more remote habitations, who boarded in the house. Arrangements
were making to increase the school, by receiving
several other children into the family.

After remaining at Mr. Westall's about ten days,
I found myself well enough to return to Brazoria,
where a vessel had in the mean time arrived from
New Orleans, to take passage in her, as she was
about to sail again. Having done with Prairie travelling and white mustangs, I took advantage of an
offer I received, to sell my little horse. A gentleman,
(the same one, by the way, who had been deceived
by his well dissembled infirmity at Harrisburgh,)
who had arrived in the vessel, and being now on a
visit at Mr. Westall's proposed to purchase him, and
gave me twenty dollars for horse, saddle and bridle:
so that I received within a few dollars of what they had
cost me, though I had travelled so much. In esti-
mating the expense I had been at for horse feed too,
it would be surprising to find how little it costs to
travel in such a country.

My fevers and agues now recurred but once in
two days; and I fortunately found at Brazoria a
young physician, just arrived, who was glad to find
in me his first applicant for the purchase of medicine. I procured from him a small quantity of qui-

nine, sufficient however to put a period to my disease, but for which he made me pay ten dollars.

After waiting two or three days, I went on board the schooner early one morning, and we proceeded down the river. My weakness kept me below almost the whole time, so that nothing presented itself to my notice worthy of particular attention until our arrival at the mouth of the river, where I spent a short time on land.

Billious fevers are one of the evils the settlement of Texas has to contend with : but in a far less degree than in the most of our Southern States.

We had proceeded some distance down the river, when a boat put off from the shore bringing a number of small bags, which the owner wished to have transported to the United States, saying they contained specie, to the amount of three or four thousand dollars. The bags were all wet ; and I learnt that they had been brought from the interior under peculiar circumstances. A trader who had disposed of his goods somewhere in the northwest, and received this specie in pay, by good management had avoided paying the lawful duties at the internal custom houses which he had passed. At length, however, when he had almost reached the end of his journey, on the banks of the Trinity river he was overtaken by several Mexicans, who had some information or suspicion against him. The trader had just unloaded his mules and placed the bags of money in a small boat, in which his assistant at that moment happened to be. The latter, on discovering the Mexicans, silently pushed off, and rowed round a neighboring point, behind which he dexterously rid himself of the load, by dropping the bags into the river. Then making such observations that he might be able to recognize the spot, he proceeded leisurely on, as if nothing had happened. The trader was seized and carried off for trial, on the charge of having no *guia*, which is tantamount to a passport: but after a little imprisonment he was set at liberty. The money had been recently recovered, and was now to be shipped for the United States.

CHAPTER XXIX.

SINCE the date of my visit to Texas, several changes
have occurred, some of which have given a different
aspect to things. The chief of these I may briefly
mention before I close this volume.

I have spoken of the character of the troops of
the Mexican army at Anahuac. It may be presumed that their presence did not add to the enjoyments
of the emigrants. As an example of what sort of
men were among them, I may mention, that three
of the soldiers deserted one day just before my arrival,
and a messenger, a North American, was despatched
to bring them back. He refused to go without per-
mission to take them "dead or alive," which was
granted. He overtook the fugitives on the bank of
Turtle bayou, where they were preparing a raft to
cross the stream. On seeing their pursuers they
attempted to flee, and two cast themselves into the
water. The messenger immediately ordered his man
to fire, and one was soon shot dead in the water, and

another was wounded in the face.   He returned with his prisoners while I was at Anahuac, and gave in his laconic report with the utmost indifference—"Colonel, I have sunk one of your men and brought home the rest."

But it was not their neighbors, nor their unpromising circumstances, nor their disappointments alone from which those poor colonists had to suffer.   After the wreck of the Climax, their numbers were increased by those who arrived in her.   When I left them, the season was hastening on, when they must be exposed to disease.

Towards the end of April, the agents received written notice from Col. Bradburn, that they would be compelled to leave the country, as the company's claims could not be recognized : Gen. Teran regarding the law of the 6th of that month as decisive. That law forbade the settlement of persons from any country bordering on Mexico.   He however offered to take the emigrants off their hands, and to furnish them with land according to the terms of the colonization laws.

Among the circumstances worthy of note which occurred in the mean time, were the following: May 7th, the first products of the garden were obtained. May 13th, the corner stone of a new fort was laid by Col. Bradburn.   May 17th, after a long drought refreshing showers came on.   July 1st, green corn was first obtained.

But before this last date, sickness had commenced its ravages among the disheartened colonists. The fever came on usually with violence, and reduced the strength very much; while the uncomfortable and crowded huts in which the emigrants lived, exposed as they were to the sun, and affording a poor shelter from the weather, together with the scarcity of medicines and the want of comforts and nurses, greatly added to its violence and effects. There was a physician at Anahuac, sent out by the Union Company; and his services were generally at command; but although the agents were men of humanity and felt for the sufferers, they could not supply all the deficiencies of a hospital, medicine and nursing.

On the 7th of July, out of one hundred and forty persons at Anahuac exclusive of the soldiers, twenty-four were on the sick list. On the 25th there had been five deaths, and the huts had been hospitals for three weeks. I copy the following melancholy note, from a memorandum made on the spot.

"Anahuac, July 28th. Our little burying ground increases in size rapidly. The first grave was dug on the 9th of June, and now there are twelve graves in it. The hottest day: thermometer at noon $97\frac{1}{2}$°."

Two able bodied men, sailors, who had been engaged to carry the surveyor's chain, and were called the chain boys, after having received a few articles of clothing in New-York, came out with the rest, and fell among the victims to the climate.

What added to their trying circumstances, was the unfeeling manner in which the Mexican authorities proceeded in cases of the decease of an alien.   They would immediately seize the property, and dispose of it at auction, for the account of the government.   This was done with little appearance of sympathy.   The clothes of the poorest emigrants were thus taken and disposed of, even to their shirts.   One young man from the West Indies, who had visited the country for his health, and died of the consumption, received from several of the agents all the kindness and attention which they had the power of affording, as they sincerely felt for his situation ; and his grave was protected with a neat fence and marked with a red cedar plank, shaped and lettered as a monument.   His effects, however, were all seized and sold, so that nothing was left even as a memento for his friends.

Cooler weather occurred on the 11th, but seemed only to increase the sickness.   On the 23d of August, Col. Bradburn gave the agents a written and peremptory order to dissolve themselves as a company by the 1st of September ; and on the following days they gave notice to the emigrants of their intention to discharge them.   All except one ultimately came forward, received a discharge and resigned their contracts, on being furnished with provisions for the remainder of the year, and such implements as could be spared.   They then sold the remaining property of the company on the best terms they could.

On my return to N. York, I got from the Trustees of the Land Company neither remuneration nor sympathy for my fruitless expense and disappointments. One of their seven agents died a short time after his return, from the effects of the climate of Texas, after compounding for a trifling sum. They claimed 10 dollars a month for above ten months, and a *labor* of land for every two months' service, acknowledging the receipt of about 90 dollars each. The Trustees offered to pay for the land at ten cents an acre. One of the agents obtained a verdict for about 1500 dollars, and another, in three trials, got verdicts for something less. Evidence stated that the Company had disposed of above six millions of acres in script some months ago. No late attempt that I have heard of has been made to settle their lands.

When General Santa Anna, in 1832, took up arms against Bustamente the Vice-President, and headed the revolution in favor of liberal principles, the American colonists in Texas were naturally inclined to support him They formed a company called the Santa Anna Guards and sailed against the Mexican troops at the mouth of the Brazos. After a skirmish they occupied the post, and then went to Anahuac, which capitulated. Colonel Bradburn, however, re-entered the town after they had retired, alleging that they had not adhered to the terms. Colonel Austin was afterwards arrested, on a charge of plotting to separate Texas from the Republic, and is still detained at Mexico.

The Cholera raged to a considerable degree in Texas in the year 1832. Several of the families which I had visited suffered deep afflictions, in the loss of one or more members; and among the persons by whom I had been treated with kindness, who were numbered among the victims, were Mr. Westall and his son, Mr. John Austin, and several others.

The Congress of the United Mexican States, on the 28th of April, 1832, repealed the 38th article of the law of 1825, which offered to any unmarried man or family a quarter of a league of land, if cultivators merely, and a league if cultivators and raisers of stock, but without interfering with grants before made.

The effect of the law forbidding the settlement of persons from adjacent countries—(that is the United States,) was also soon arrested.

The following are stated to be some of the principal provisions of the new colonization law, relating to foreign settlers. The law of April 6, 1830, forbidding settlers from the United States is repealed. A foreign settler shall receive two *labors*, unless the land is susceptible of irrigation, and then one *labor*, and a supply of water. If he has above 100 cattle or horses, and 600 sheep, half a league. A trifling consideration only, is in any case to be paid. The settler will be free from taxes for ten years, unless in case of invasion. He may bequeath his land, even if unoccupied, but not otherwise alienate it until after occupation for six years. It is designed to form close settlements of 30 families. I do not know that the old terms are otherwise changed. I presume a settler must become a citizen and a Roman Catholic.

A new revolution occurred in Mexico in June 1834, the influence of which, if it should become general and lasting, would doubtless be unfavorable to the settlement of North Americans in the country. Gen. Santa Anna, after appearing to favor the very liberal plan of general reformation proposed by the Congress, prorogued it, and finally prevented its reassembling by stationing troops at the doors of their chambers. He has the priests and monarchists in his favor, and will probably involve the country in another protracted civil war. Had the late Congress, with the Vice President, Farias, succeeded in their patriotic wishes, religious toleration would have been established, the convents would have been suppressed, and other important improvements introduced, demanded by the nature of a republican government.

The colonization of Texas has been proceeding, and in some parts, as I have understood, with considerable activity. Many have gone of late to Austin's upper colony. The settlers continue to be principally persons from the Southern and Western States.

Texas is every year traversed by numbers of our enterprising countrymen. Report has recently reached New-York, that a young man of this city, within a few months, penetrated to the head spring of the Rio Bravo, after a long and perilous journey among the Indians, and was the first white man who ever reached the spot.

A person lately returned from a land journey through Texas, states, that the Irish colonies about Aransaso Bay, in the western part, were rapidly filling up by settlers from Ireland. Vessels are often also advertised as about to sail for that part from the United States.

The distances across Texas, according to common estimate, are as follows: From Trinidad river, (on the Nacogdoches route,) to San Felipe, 110 miles; thence to the Colorado, 35; thence to the Navedad, 37; La Baca, 9; Guadaloupe, 35; Lababi, 25; Nueces, 60; from Nueces to Matamoras, 200 miles; thirty nights to sleep out—only four estates on the way.

The Comanches Indians still occasionally come down to the coast west of Austin's Colony, and with some other tribes, inspire terror; but travelling with arms is thought safe.

METEOROLOGICAL JOURNAL,

Kept at Anahuac, in March, April, May, June, July, August and September, 1831.

MARCH.

Date	Morning	Noon	Evening	Winds	Weather	Date	Morning	Noon	Evening	Winds	Weather
1	80	92	78	s.	Pleasant.	17	46	61	60	s. w.	Clear & pleasant.
2	78	92	74	s.	Light w'ds & pl't.	18	48	51	50	s.	Pleasant.
3	70	76	70	s. e.	Cloudy.	19	60	61	60	n. w.	Cold.
4	68	70	70	s.w.	do.	20	60	65	60	—	Clear & pleasant.
5	68	68	65	s. e.	Pleasant.	21	47	67	57	e.	do.
6	46	69	46	n.	Wind high & cold.	22	68	69	68	do.	Cloudy, high wi'd.
7	44	64	58	n.w.	Pleasant.	23	69	74	72	do.	do. do. & some r'in.
8	47	66	58	n.w.	do.	24	60	76	72	—	Very pl't & warm.
9	48	68	60	n. e.	do.	25	66	68	61	e.	Rain.
10	60	65	58	n.	do.	26	70	80	70	s. e.	Pleasant.
11	65	70	60	s. e.	do.	27	69	75	72	w.	do.
12	62	65	60	—	Clo'dy, rai'g. at 11.	28	70	30	70	e.	do.
13	70	75	70	—	----	29	54	68	58	n.w.	Clo'y & high wind.
14	70	78	69	s. w.	Pleasant.	30	58	73	68	w.	Pleasant.
15	68	73	70	—	Cha'ble, th'r & r'n.	31	65	76	72	s. e.	do.
16	48	63	62	n.w.	Sq'y, rain, cl.& cd.						

APRIL.

Date	Morning	Noon	Evening	Winds	Weather	Date	Morning	Noon	Evening	Winds	Weather
1	72	74	74	s. e.	Cloudy.	14	60	62	59	s. e.	Pleasant.
2	72	80	74	do.	do.	15	60	69	66	n. w. / pm.s e.	do. P. M. heavy rain.
3	80	76	67	do.	do.	16	68	76	70	s. e.	Pleasant.
4	50	62	68	n. w.	Pleasant.	17	66	78	72	do.	do. and calm.
5	48	62	58	do.	do.	18	74	83	82	n. n. e.	Pleasant.
6	62	65	68	s. e.	do.	19	73	78	74		. do.
7	70	72	72	s. s. e. / p. m. / n. w.	Foggy, r'n. P. M. severe gale & cold.	20	72	80	74	s. e.	do.
						21	73	80	74	do.	Cloudy.
8	44	54	54	n. w.	St'g w'd & p't	22	74	33	77	do.	Pleasant.
9	47	60	62	—	Plea't & calm.	23	77	80	70	do.	do.
10	57	70	68	s. w.	Pleasant.	24	62	76	68	n. w.	do.
11	57	76	72	—	do. and calm.	25	57	76	72	e.	do.
12	62	73	65	s. s. e.	Clo'y & very windy. Evening gale.	26	58	77	68	w.	do.
						27	62	76	66	s. e.	do.
						28	62	76	66	do.	do.
13	62	67	64	—	Cl'y, violent wind & rain cold& foggy	29	68	78	70	do.	do.
						30	68	78	70	do.	do.

Wind southerly 22 days out of 30.

MAY.

Date	Morning	Noon	Evening	Winds	Weather	Date	Morning	Noon	Evening	Winds	Weather
1	77	82	77	S.	Pleasant	15	76	74	70	do.PM. } S. W.	do P. M. rain.
2	76	96	82	E.	do	16	64	6:	60	S. E.	Pl'nt. night } heavy sh'er.
3	70	81	76	S. E.	do	17	55	70	66	N. W.	Pleasant
4	72	82	77	do.	Cloudy	18	60	78	68	do.	do
5	72	81	80	do.	do	19	66	86	76	S. E.	do'
6	78	78	80	S. E. 11 o'clock } S. W.	Pleasant	20	72	84	70	do.	do
7	64	76	74	N.	do and warm.	21	68	87	80	do.	do and warm.
8	62	80	74	N. W.	Pleasant	22	61	87	90	S. W.	do P.M. th'r. and rain.
9	64	80	74	S.E. 1 P M. S. }	do	23	71	86	78	N.	Cloudy
10	62	80	74	do.	Pleasant, 11 o'clock th'r. and rain.	24	66	78	77	do.	Pleasant
11	68	84	72	do. 11 o'clock } S. W.	do	25	72	86	79	S. W.	do
12	72	74	74	S. E.	Pleasant	26	73	88	79	do.	do
13	74	84	68	do.	do	27	73	33	70	S. E.	do, rain.
14	72	84	76	do.	do	28	74	82	70	E. S. E.	Pleasant
						29	72	87	78	S. E.	do
						30	70	87	72	E. S. E.	do
						31	80	87	73	do.	do

Wind southerly 24 days.

JUNE.

Date	Morning	Noon	Evening	Winds	Weather	Date	Morning	Noon	Evening	Winds	Weather
1	70	87	78	S. E.	P. M. ch'ble } pleasant.	15	75	88	80	S. E.	Cloudy
2	73	86	78	do	P. M. ch'ble } pleasant.	16	75	86	82	do	Showers
3	74	87	82	do	Pleasant	17	74	86	73	s. s. w.	Heavy sho'rs
4	72	87	79	N.	do	18	70	86	73	Variable	Cloudy
5	70	87	87	S. E.	do	19	74	86	73	—	Rain
6	79	84	82	do	do	20	78	84	82	s. w.	Pleasant
7	78	84	81	s. s. e.	Pleasant	21	74	88	82	S. E.	—
8	79	84	80	s.	—	22	77	86	92	s. s. w.	Hazy
9	76	87	78	S. E.	—	23	80	86	82	s. w.	—
10	73	87	83	—	—	24	78	89	81	S. E.	Fair
11	75	87	85	N.	—	25	76	89	93	s.	Evening th'r.
12	78	88	84	—	—	26	73	86	84	s. w.	Rain in mor'g
13	72	90	84	W.	—	27	72	86	82	N. N. W.	Fair
14	78	86	79	S.	—	28	69	83	92	N. W.	—
						29	71	86	80	S.	—
						30	72	86	80	S. E.	—

Average Heat. 74d. 36m.—86d 0m.—80d. 44m.—Twenty days pleasant weather. Winds from S. and S. E. It may perhaps be worthy of remark, that during this month, gentle land breezes have prevailed every morning until about 8 o'clock, after which a sea breeze until about sunset, which may be considered the prevaling wind through the summer months.

JULY.

Date	Morning	Noon	Evening	Winds	Weather	Date	Morning	Noon	Evening	Winds	Weather
1	76	88	84	N. E.	Fair	17	76	87	84	s. s. w.	Pleasant
2	72	88	84	S. W.	—	18	78	90	82	s. w.	Clear
3	72	90	84	S.	—	19	80	90	84	—	Thun'r & rain
4	74	92	84	Calm	Mrn.Showery	20	78	91	84	s. e.	Shower
5	82	92	86	s. by E.	Pleasant	21	78	84	82	—	
6	80	92	86	s. w.	—	22	80	87	82	—	
7	80	93	89		—	23	80	84	81	e.w.by s.	Pleasant
8	80	92	90	; s.	—	24	80	86	84	s.	—
9	78	94	88	s. w.	—	25	78	88	84	s. by w.	—
10	78	92	80	Variable	R'n & Thnd'r	26	82	39	36	s. w.	—
11	74	86	80	N. E.	Fair	27	80	89	8:	—	
12	74	83	80	—	Showers	28	80	86	88	N.	Part of the day showry
13	71	85	84	—	Cloudy	29	80	90	88	s.	Clear
14	74	88	81	—		30	80	89	88	s. e.	—
15	80	88	80	Variable	Showers	31	84	39	86	s.	
16	78	79	76	s. s. w.	Rain						

REMARKS.—Average heat, 81d. 13m—88d. 38m.—84d. 0m.—Many showers this month; very high tides. On the 5th heavy rain in the morning. On the 10th, heavy squall with rain, thunder, and lightning.

AUGUST.

Date	Morning	Noon	Evening	Winds	Weather	Date	Morning	Noon	Evening	Winds	Weather
1	78	89	85	s. e.	Fair	17	80	88	87	N. W.	Hazy
2	78	87	86	—		18	84	89	57	—	Clear
3	79	96	85	Variable	Showers	19	83	88	82	s. w.	Light show'rs
4	79	89	85	Calm	Fair	20	82	88	84	—	Fair
5	78	89	85	s. e.		21	80	84	80	s.	Hazy
6	82	86	84	Variable	Cl'y & show's	22	78	83	82	N. E.	Fair
7	73	77	80	N. E.	Pleasant	23	75	80	80	—	—
8	68	80	72	- -		24	70	78	77	—	—
9	66	79	71	—		25	71	81	81	—	—
10	70	80	79	—		26	74	87	80	—	
11	75	86	83	—	Cloudy	27	73	83	84	—	Flying Clo'ds
12	76	84	83	E. N. E.	Clear	28	76	85	80	—	Cloudy & rain
13	80	84	81	N.E.by E.	Rain	29	76	77	74	N. GALE.	Showery
14	79	82	82	s.	Cloudy	30	75	85	84	s.	Clear
15	76	81	81	s. e.	Showers	31	78	84	82	s. e.	Hazy
16	78	85	85	N. E.							

REMARKS.—Average heat, 76d. 23m.—84d. 19m.—81d. 36m. Easterly winds prevailing.

SEPTEMBER.

Date	Morning	Noon	Evening	Winds	Weather	Date	Morning	Noon	Evening	Winds	Weather
1	76	84	84	w.	Clear	11	78	82	80	Variable	Rain
2	80	86	83	s.	Hazy	12	75	80	77	N. E.	Light Show's
3	76	85	83	—	Clear	13	73	80	80	S. E.	Cloudy
4	77	85	82	—	—	14	70	78	76	—	Clear
5	76	86	81	—	—	15	76	82	78	N. E.	—
6	75	86	82	—	—	16	76	81	78	—	Cloudy
7	78	86	83	—	—	17	74	82	78	—	Hazy
8	80	86	81	—	—	18	69	76	76	S. E.	Clear
9	78	87	84	—	—	19	66	74	70	—	Fair
10	80	86	82	—	—	20	68	76	72		—

REMARKS—Average heat, 75*d*. 3*m*.—82*d*. 7*m*.—79*d*. 30*m*.—Winds S and S. E. about two-thirds of the time.

CHAPTER XXVII.

Travels north of San Felipe, (*continued.*)—North-west corner of Austin's Colony.—Wild horses, deer, buffalo.—Dread of Indians.— The Colorado river.—Returning.—Appearance of strangers on a Prairie.—Rencontre.—Lose our way.—San Felipe.

ONE of my companions had accompanied me further than the others, because he wished to inspect a tract of land he had obtained near the north-western corner of Austin's Colony. Beyond that angle we did not design to go ; and on approaching the Colorado river near that point, we regarded it as the end of our excursion. The last colonist we found in that direction, was a man who had emigrated some years before from Pennsylvania ; and had acquired a comfortable property in a short time through the luxuriance of the soil. He was surrounded, though at no inconsiderable distances, by settlers from different parts of the United States. We saw that we were in a wilder country, so far as related to game and wild animals, than any we had seen ; for having gradually arrived among a thin population, and approached somewhat nearer the regions inhabited by Indians, we occasionally perceived the tracks of buffalo, which are not uncommon there, and heard of wild hogs, bears and panthers. One of the swine we had seen dead at a house at which we had stopped a few days before. It had been shot, and though not large, appeared like rather a formidable animal, being armed with tusks of considerable length, which curled back from his under jaw. The animal was greyish, and of a disagreeable aspect. According to common report they have sometimes attacked men.

Our host having proposed an excursion to the very extremity of the colony, we accepted it, and, mounting our horses, accompanied him on a ride over a very pleasant, though unoccupied region. We were still annoyed by flies. We saw deer and mustangs in herds, and frequently noticed the fresh marks of buffalo, which are often killed hereabouts. We had left our guns at San Felipe, considering them almost as useless as burdensome; but we had our pistols with us, and our new companion went better armed with his rifle. We soon perceived that he was under constant apprehension of Indians, and that an unceremonious fashion which prevailed, of shooting down red men wherever they were found, was the order of the day. He recounted tales of savage murders perpetrated on settlers and travellers at different times; and would often interrupt himself or us to say: "How I would shoot an Indian if he should jump out of the bushes yonder!" He would look, and act too, as if he really expected to meet every moment with such an unwelcome traveller.

We now began to think we had not done wisely in leaving our guns at San Felipe : for it seemed as if a settler, well acquainted with the country, and heretofore engaged in savage warfare, could not entertain such apprehensions of an enemy unless there was some real danger. We had before never admitted a thought of fear from such a quarter : but now, the more we thought of the vast regions north of us, free to the passage of a wily and rapid foe, the thinness of the population around us, and the defenceless condition of the frontier, the more we began to participate in the feelings of our host, and to scrutinize the groves and thickets as we passed them, with uncommon care. However, we discovered nothing to alarm our fears any further ; and, as we were to turn our faces for San Felipe the next day, we congratulated ourselves that we should have no reason for further apprehension.

The direction we had taken, (road there was none,) brought us at length to the left bank of the Colorado river, there a small stream at this season, though sometimes, like the other Texas rivers, it is raised to a considerable height. We turned and followed down its course for some distance, and afterwards leaving it, we returned to the house of our new friend.

We were now at the north-western corner of what is commonly called Austin's first colony, though, as I have elsewhere remarked, this term is to be understood here in a very limited sense. North of it lies a smaller tract of land, called Austin's New Colony, beyond which is another, called Williams and Austin's, where as yet few settlers had been introduced. The nature of the surface, the quality of the soil, the productions and climate, as I was informed, continue much the same for a great distance beyond, and must hereafter invite numerous settlers, when circumstances shall be more favorable.

The liberal and tolerant views of the government of Mexico at the time when the first part of this book was writing, were such as to encourage the hope that our countrymen might be admitted without being required to renounce Protestantism. In that case, if the country had continued to enjoy peace and prosperity, and land had still been given to foreign emigrants on the same terms, no doubt these extensive and attractive regions would have become rapidly occupied; being brought into powerful competition with the wild lands within our own borders, and particularly those in the adjacent states. But until some sure guarantee is given, there can be no sufficient security offered to Protestants, that they or their children will be allowed to worship God according to the dictates of their conciences. A revolution has recently occurred, which has given the priests and anti-reformers the ascendancy.

The following morning we set off on our return. Having got some information concerning the number, situation and bearings of the settlements near our